READY TO WORK
Winning at the Job Game

Project Editor
Frances A. Wiser

Developed by
Contemporary Books, Inc.
and
Visual Education Corporation
Princeton, New Jersey

CONTEMPORARY BOOKS
CHICAGO

Library of Congress Cataloging-in-Publication Data

Wiser, Fran.
    Ready to work : winning at the job game / Fran Wiser.
       p.   cm.
   ISBN 0-8092-4099-8
    1. Vocational guidance.   2. Career development.   I. Title.
HF5381.W774   1990   90-48667
                                                                    CIP

Cover photo: © Michael Slaughter, courtesy of Graham Plating Company, Inc., Chicago, Illinois.

Pages iii (Sections 1, 2, 3), iv (Sections 4, 6, 7), v (Sections 8, 9, 10), 1, 13, 23, 37, 39, 43, 48, 51, 69, 83, 91, 104, 109, 111: Robert Bruschini/Studio B; pages iv (Section 5), 58, 71, 95: Gary Mattie; page 4: Visual Education Corporation

This book is an educational book. Names, characters, places, and incidents are used solely to illustrate the sections contained herein and should not be considered real or factual. The persons portrayed in photographs are models. Their actions, motivations, and dialogue are entirely fictional. Any resemblance to actual persons, living or dead, and actual events or locales is entirely coincidental.

Copyright © 1991 by Contemporary Books, Inc.
All rights reserved

No part of this publication may be reproduced, stored in a retrieval system, or transmitted in any form or by any means, without the prior written permission of the publisher.

Published by Contemporary Books, Inc.
Two Prudential Plaza, Chicago, Illinois 60601-6790
Manufactured in the United States of America
International Standard Book Number: 0-8092-4099-8

Published simultaneously in Canada by
Fitzhenry & Whiteside
195 Allstate Parkway
Markham, Ontario L3R 4T8
Canada

Editorial Director
Caren Van Slyke

Assistant Editorial Director
Mark Boone

Project Editor
Frances A. Wiser

Editor
Suzanne Eckert

Editorial Assistant
Carol Ciaston

Cover Design
Lois Koehler

Production Consultants
Jean Farley Brown
Norma Fioretti

Reviewers
Karin Evans
Kathy Osmus

Writers
Natalie Goldstein
Cheryl Morrison
Karen Theroux

Production Supervisor
Anita Crandall

Designers
Max Crandall
Susan Riley

Illustrator
Bill Colrus

Photography
Toby Mosko

CONTENTS

Introduction   vi

1 GETTING READY FOR WORK 1

Learning About Yourself
LearningAbout Your Strengths
What Work Experience Do You Have?
Learning About Work Tasks
Getting a Social Security Card

2 FINDING A JOB LEAD 13

Talking with People You Know
Answering Help-Wanted Signs
Understanding Help-Wanted Ads
Blind Ads
Using Other Sources in the Job Hunt
Using the Telephone
Contacting State Employment Services

3 APPLYING YOURSELF 23

Applying in Person
Making Notes for Application Forms
How to Fill Out Job Application Forms
Applying by Letter
How to Write an Application Letter
Writing a Resume
Following Up on Job Interviews

4 Q & A: THE JOB INTERVIEW 37

Knowing What to Expect
Finding Out About the Job
Preparing Questions
Questions You Can Expect
Listening and Watching as You Practice
Showing a Positive Attitude
How to Practice for Interviews
Preparing to Take Tests
A Few More Details to Consider
How to Plan Your Time

5 A WINNING INTERVIEW 48

Making a Lasting Impression
Interviewing Do's and Don'ts
Answering Difficult Questions
An Applicant's Rights
How to End the Interview
How to Follow Up on the Interview

6 I'LL TAKE IT! 58

The Right Job for You
Working Hours
A Job's Location
What Does It Pay?
Payment Methods
Job Benefits
Types of Benefits
Job Costs
A Job's Future

7 THE WORLD OF WORK 69

Day One
Company Policies
Understanding a Form W-4
Using Time Cards and Timesheets
Insurance Forms

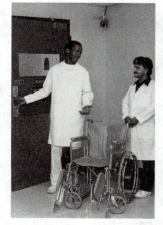

How to Compare Health Insurance
Getting Your First Paycheck
Understanding a Form W-2

8 A JUGGLING ACT 83

Balancing Work and Personal Demands
Being a Good Time Manager
Arranging Child Care
Helping Low-Income Families Get Child Care
Managing Your Money
Handling Illness
Dealing with Stress

9 KNOWING YOUR RIGHTS 95

Employees Have Rights
Employers Have Rights Too
The Right to a Safe Workplace
Freedom from Sexual Harassment
Discrimination on the Job
The Right to Privacy

10 SUCCEEDING ON THE JOB 104

Tips for Succeeding
You and Your Supervisor
You and Your Co-Workers
Handling Performance Reviews
How Are Workers Evaluated?
Asking for a Raise or Promotion
Are You Promotable?
Changing Jobs
When It's Time to Leave

WORDS TO KNOW 116

ANSWER KEY 119

INTRODUCTION

How do you get a job? Once you have a job, how do you succeed at it? *Ready to Work: Winning at the Job Game* is designed to help you develop the skills you need to get the job you want and succeed at it.

Ready to Work can help you no matter what stage of the job-search game you're at. The book is divided into 10 sections.

- If you're not sure what kind of work you're suited for, Section 1 can help you pinpoint your interests and abilities.
- Sections 2 and 3 suggest where and how you can look for a job.
- Sections 4 and 5 explain interviews—how to get ready for them and what to do when you go on them.
- Section 6 discusses how to choose the job that's right for you.

Ready to Work: Winning at the Job Game can also be useful to you once you have a job.

- In Sections 7 and 8, for example, you will learn how to adjust to work as well as how to balance job and family demands.
- Section 9 covers your legal rights at work.
- Finally, Section 10 shows you how to succeed at work.

Each section of *Ready to Work* opens with a story about a person who has faced a job-related issue and dealt with it successfully. The content of each section is designed to help you learn job skills and then give you practice in using these skills. For example, in Section 3, you will learn how to write an application letter. Later in the same section, you will have the chance to write an actual letter.

Within each section, words that will be useful to know are shown in a **darker type.** At the end of each section, you will have a chance to apply what you have learned in four different types of exercises. Many of these exercises require you to put yourself in someone else's shoes to answer questions or solve problems. That way, you learn what to do when faced with similar situations in your own job search.

There is an answer key at the end of this book for exercises that have specific, correct answers. However, many of the questions and exercises are based on your personal experiences, ideas, and opinions. Of course, there are no answer key references for those questions.

We hope that *Ready to Work* will help you better understand your interests and abilities and to make the most of yourself in today's job market.

SECTION ONE
GETTING READY FOR WORK

Dave sat across from Mr. King, a job counselor for his town's employment program. He liked Mr. King, but he wasn't sure that anybody could help him find the right job.

"I just don't know what I want to do," Dave said. "I don't have any skills."

"Everybody has skills," Mr. King said. "Why don't you start by telling me what you like doing?"

"I like playing softball and being with my family—helping them out or having fun."

"How do you help your family?" Mr. King asked.

"I help with the cleaning and the shopping," Dave said. "See, my mom and dad both work. And they need me to give them a hand whenever I can."

"It seems to me that you like being with people," Mr. King said.

"Yes, I do," Dave said.

"And do you like cleaning?"

"I don't mind doing that," Dave said. "Because I like having things in their place."

"And if you play softball, you're obviously in good shape," Mr. King commented.

"Well," Mr. King said, "you can put those skills and interests together to get a job. Have you ever thought about working at a hotel?"

"A hotel?" Dave asked.

"Sure," Mr. King said. "You could help people by carrying their bags. And there's a good future in hotel work. Does that interest you?"

"It sounds great," Dave said.

There were many things that Dave had to think about before he could decide what kind of job he wanted to look for. When you try to decide what kind of job you want, you should think about:

- how you like to spend your time
- what matters most to you about a job
- your talents and skills
- your work experience

LEARNING ABOUT YOURSELF

Mr. King asked Dave questions about his likes and dislikes. By answering the questions, Dave learned about some of his skills and interests. He also learned that he can use those skills and interests to choose a job that he might like.

In much the same way, you will answer questions throughout this section. You will use the answers to learn more about yourself and the kinds of jobs that would probably be right for you. There are no right or wrong answers to the questions in this section. Only you need to know your answers.

When you answer the questions, be honest. Your answers will tell you what's important to you. They will help point out which kinds of jobs may be best for you.

Let's start with questions about your interests. Your **interests** are the activities that you enjoy and the things you like to talk about or read about. You are more likely to enjoy your work if it involves a subject or an activity you're interested in.

What Are Your Interests?

Your responses to the items listed below help you zero in on your interests. After each statement, write *yes* if it applies to you or *no* if it does not.

1. I like working with my hands. _____
2. I enjoy spending time outdoors. _____
3. I like working with machinery. _____
4. I like solving puzzles. _____
5. I enjoy traveling. _____
6. I like to work with numbers. _____

What Are Your Values?

The parts of a job that are most important to you make up your **work values.** These may include what the workplace is like, how fast-paced the work is, and so on. For example, some people can't work well in a noisy office. Other people think that noise makes an office interesting. You should consider these and many other work values when you look for a job.

Your responses to the items that follow will help you zero in on your work values. After each statement, write *yes* or *no*.

1. I like doing the same thing over and over. _____
2. I like to spend a lot of time with other people. _____

3. I enjoy helping other people. _____
4. I like physical activity. _____
5. I like to follow directions. _____
6. I work best in quiet, peaceful surroundings. _____

LEARNING ABOUT YOUR STRENGTHS

Learning about your interests and values can help you decide what you want from a job. But you also need to consider what you have to offer.

When Dave first met with Mr. King, he didn't think he had any skills. Mr. King helped Dave see what some of his skills were. Like Dave, you have **strengths** to offer employers. Your strengths can be grouped into:

- talents
- basic skills
- technical skills
- background skills
- education and training

Everyone has certain **talents.** Your talents are shown by what you can learn or do easily. For example, you may have a talent for fixing things. If so, it's probably not hard for you to learn to fix new things. If you are aware of your talents, you can figure out which skills you can learn most easily.

Skills require a certain amount of learning and practice. Repairing a car, for example, takes skill. No matter how much talent you have, you can't repair a car without the skills you learn through training and experience.

Most employers expect you to have **basic skills** before they hire you. These basic skills are reading, writing, and doing math. For example, if you were applying for a job as a cashier, your employer would require you to be able to add and subtract.

You probably have more skills than you think. When people list their skills, they often list only their basic skills or their **technical** (TEK•nih•kul) **skills.** Technical skills are those used in doing certain tasks, such as typing, operating a cash register, or operating a forklift.

In addition, most adults also have **background skills.** These are skills that are used in many areas of life. They can also help you on the job. For example, if you've taken care of a home and children, then you have many kinds of background skills. You've shown that you can take care of others, manage your time and money, and organize people and things.

All of your skills can be counted as **qualifications** (kwahl•uh•fuh•KAY•shuns) for jobs. For example, if you are a good driver and have first-aid training, you might qualify for a job as a paramedic.

Schools and training programs can provide skills you need for certain jobs. When you complete schools or programs, you receive diplomas or certificates. They can be used to show you are qualified for certain jobs.

The next list of questions will help you identify your talents, skills, education, and training. Your answers will help you figure out what kinds of jobs you are likely to do well.

If you've taken care of a home and children, then your skills include managing time and money and organizing people and things.

 What Are Your Strengths?

Talents

What kinds of things are you good at? (Examples: repairing broken things, dealing with children.)

_____

_____

Skills

What basic skills do you have that you can use in a job? (Examples: doing math, reading, writing.)

_____

_____

What technical skills do you have that you can use in a job? (Examples: cooking, speaking a foreign language, repairing engines.)

_____

_____

_____

What background skills do you have that you can use in a job? (Examples: keeping track of details, using physical strength, taking care of children.)

_____

_____

Section One

Education and Training

What diplomas or certificates do you have? (Examples: a high school or general equivalency diploma [GED].)

_____

_____

_____

Do you have any other special training? (Examples: a community college class in bookkeeping, a course in auto mechanics.)

_____

_____

_____

WHAT WORK EXPERIENCE DO YOU HAVE?

When you try to show an employer that you can do a job, the best proof you can offer is past work experience. In fact, any work experience you have may help you in your job search.

Your work experience includes jobs that you held in stores, offices, and factories. It also includes work you may have done in your neighborhood. For example, if you have earned money painting houses, caring for children, or mowing lawns, that is part of your work experience. Volunteer work, such as serving food to the homeless or teaching a Sunday school class, is also work experience.

By looking at your work experience, you can learn about the kinds of work you enjoy. You can also learn about the kinds of skills you have used in jobs. In fact, employers often ask for certain work experience as a requirement for jobs. For example, you may need one to three years of experience working in retail sales to get a job as a salesclerk in a department store.

LEARNING ABOUT WORK TASKS

Jobs usually involve specific types of work tasks. Work tasks can focus on four things:

- **Data.** Some jobs focus heavily on data (DAYT•uh), or information, such as facts, numbers, papers, and files. Bookkeepers and secretaries work with data; so do bank tellers and data-entry clerks.
- **Ideas.** Some jobs focus on finding new ways to express ideas or solve problems. People in these jobs include artists, writers, performers, and scientists.
- **People.** Helping, teaching, and caring for people is the focus of some jobs. People in these jobs include nurses, teachers, and salespeople.
- **Objects.** Some workers spend most of their time with machines, tools, or materials. The people who do this include carpenters, cooks, and repair technicians.

Most jobs include some of each of these work tasks. For example, most secretarial duties involve working with data, but secretaries also work with people. Secretaries may also work with ideas (to solve problems) and with

Getting Ready for Work   5

objects (such as dictation machines, computers, or word processors). Even though jobs may include many types of work tasks, most still focus on one. Finding out which work tasks you like best can help you identify jobs that you may enjoy.

Which Work Tasks Interest You?

The questions below will help you identify which work tasks interest you the most. This will help you pick out jobs that you might like.

Answer the questions to see which tasks you like the best. Then read the job lists below the questions for job ideas.

Data Yes No

1. Do you like to work with facts? ☐ ☐
2. Do you like to work with numbers? ☐ ☐
3. Do you like to keep records? ☐ ☐
4. Do you like to work with papers and files? ☐ ☐

Job Ideas: bank teller, postal clerk, secretary, statistical clerk, typist/word processor

Ideas Yes No

1. Do you like to put your ideas on paper? ☐ ☐
2. Do you like to draw, paint, or design? ☐ ☐
3. Do you like to solve problems? ☐ ☐
4. Do you like to study nature or investigate the unknown? ☐ ☐

Job Ideas: artist, florist, painter, photographer

People Yes No

1. Do you like to help people? ☐ ☐
2. Do you like to give information to people? ☐ ☐
3. Do you like to teach? ☐ ☐
4. Do you like to take care of people? ☐ ☐

Job Ideas: corrections officer, counter clerk, paramedic, nurse, receptionist, salesperson, travel agent

Objects Yes No

1. Do you like to take care of machines? ☐ ☐
2. Do you like to handle supplies or equipment? ☐ ☐
3. Do you like to operate or drive equipment? ☐ ☐
4. Do you like to repair machines or equipment? ☐ ☐

Job Ideas: auto-body repairer, cook, farmer, kitchen helper, mechanic, taxi driver

Look back over your answers. Which work task had the most *yes* answers?   data   ideas   people   objects   (*circle one*)

Which work task had the most *no* answers?   data   ideas   people   objects   (*circle one*)

Which Jobs Interest You?

Read over the chart of nine common jobs on page 8. Choose three occupations from the chart that interest you. Write the job titles of those occupations on the lines below. Then answer the questions about each occupation.

Job title #1: _____

What interests you about this job?
_____
_____

Do you meet any of the qualifications for this job? _____

If so, which ones? _____
_____

Does the job relate to any of your interests, strengths, or work experience? _____

If so, how? _____
_____

Job title #2: _____

What interests you about this job?
_____
_____
_____

Do you meet any of the qualifications for this job? _____

If so, which ones? _____
_____

Does the job relate to any of your interests, strengths, or work experience? _____

If so, how? _____
_____

Job title #3: _____

What interests you about this job?
_____
_____
_____

Do you meet any of the qualifications for this job? _____

If so, which ones? _____
_____

Does the job relate to any of your interests, strengths, or work experience? _____

If so, how? _____
_____

If any of these jobs that match your interests also match your qualifications, you might want to consider them as possible future jobs.

Getting Ready for Work

NINE COMMON JOBS

The chart below includes nine jobs and gives details about them.

OCCUPATION	WORK TASK	ABILITIES	QUALIFICATIONS
Auto-body repairer	Objects	Using hand tools, having physical strength	High school diploma preferred but not necessary; a certificate from a trade school is helpful
Cook or kitchen helper	Objects	Cooking, working quickly, doing several activities at once	Entry-level jobs have no education requirements, but people with high school diplomas and post–high school training are most likely to advance
Corrections officer	People	Giving instruction, helping people solve problems	High school diploma; additional training in psychology or related fields preferred
Counter clerk	People	Taking customer orders, working a cash register, making change	High school diploma preferred but not required
Florist	Ideas	Flair for color and design	High school diploma preferred
Paramedic	People	Using medical equipment, handling stress	High school diploma; training in emergency care
Photographer	Ideas	Artistic ability, patience, accuracy, attention to detail	High school diploma preferred but not required; photography courses helpful
Statistical clerk	Data	Attention to detail, working with numbers, using a computer keyboard	High school diploma; courses in typing, data processing, and bookkeeping are helpful
Typist/Word processor	Data	Using a typewriter or computer keyboard, accuracy, attention to detail, good spelling and grammar	High school graduate

GETTING A SOCIAL SECURITY CARD

Before you start to look for a job, you may need to take care of a few details. One of them is getting a Social Security card. The Social Security Administration assigns you a number which is printed on your Social Security card.

All workers must have a Social Security number. You need your number in order to fill out job applications, enroll in schools, and file your income tax returns. Any people, such as your children, who are listed as dependents on your income tax returns must also have Social Security numbers.

When you have a job, both you and your employer pay into the Social Security fund each month. This entitles you to certain benefits, such as money after retirement. The government uses your Social Security number to figure out what benefits you are entitled to and how much you should be paid.

To get a Social Security card, go to a Social Security office and fill out an application. To find the office nearest you, look in the phone book under United States Government, then under the subheading Social Security. If the phone book doesn't list the address, call the office to find out where it is.

Social Security cards are free, but you must fill out an application form to get one. When you fill out an application form, you must provide proof of age, citizenship, and identity.

Most people use the following:

- their birth certificate
- one other form of identification, such as a driver's license, medical records, or school records

If you can't get an official copy of your birth certificate, you can use some other record of your birth that was made before you were five years old. This could be a record from a hospital or religious organization. You must provide original documents or official copies, not photocopies.

After filling out a form and providing documentation, you will get two Social Security cards—one to carry with you and one to keep in a safe place. If you lose both cards and you know your number, you can get replacements from the Social Security office.

Practice Filling Out a Social Security Card Application

Read the instructions that follow and fill out the application for a Social Security card on page 10.

How to complete this form

Most questions on the form are self-explanatory. The questions that need explanation are discussed on page 10. The numbers match the numbered questions on the form. <u>If you are completing this form for someone else, please answer the questions as they apply to that person.</u> Then, sign your own name.

SOCIAL SECURITY ADMINISTRATION
Application for a Social Security Card

Form Approved
OMB No. 0960-0066

INSTRUCTIONS
- Please read "How To Complete This Form."
- Print or type using black or blue ink. DO NOT USE PENCIL.
- After you complete this form, take or mail it along with the required documents to your nearest Social Security office.
- If you are completing this form for someone else, answer the questions as they apply to that person. Then, sign your name in question 16.

1. **NAME** To Be Shown On Card — FIRST / FULL MIDDLE NAME / LAST

   FULL NAME AT BIRTH IF OTHER THAN ABOVE — FIRST / FULL MIDDLE NAME / LAST

   OTHER NAMES USED

2. **MAILING ADDRESS** Do Not Abbreviate — STREET ADDRESS, APT. NO., PO BOX, RURAL ROUTE NO.

   CITY / STATE / ZIP CODE

3. **CITIZENSHIP** (Check One) — ☐ U.S. Citizen ☐ Legal Alien Allowed To Work ☐ Legal Alien Not Allowed To Work ☐ Foreign Student Allowed Restricted Employment ☐ Conditionally Legalized Alien Allowed To Work ☐ Other (See Instructions On Page 2)

4. **SEX** — ☐ Male ☐ Female

5. **RACE/ETHNIC DESCRIPTION** (Check One Only—Voluntary) — ☐ Asian, Asian-American Or Pacific Islander ☐ Hispanic ☐ Black (Not Hispanic) ☐ North American Indian Or Alaskan Native ☐ White (Not Hispanic)

6. **DATE OF BIRTH** — MONTH DAY YEAR

7. **PLACE OF BIRTH** (Do Not Abbreviate) — CITY / STATE OR FOREIGN COUNTRY

   Office Use Only — FCI

8. **MOTHER'S MAIDEN NAME** — FIRST / FULL MIDDLE NAME / LAST NAME AT HER BIRTH

9. **FATHER'S NAME** — FIRST / FULL MIDDLE NAME / LAST

10. Has the person in item 1 ever applied for or received a Social Security number before?
    ☐ Yes (If "yes", answer questions 11-13.) ☐ No (If "no", go on to question 14.) ☐ Don't Know (If "don't know", go on to question 14.)

11. Enter the Social Security number previously assigned to the person listed in item 1.
    ☐☐☐-☐☐-☐☐☐☐

12. Enter the name shown on the most recent Social Security card issued for the person listed in item 1.
    FIRST / MIDDLE / LAST

13. Enter any different date of birth if used on an earlier application for a card. — MONTH DAY YEAR

14. **TODAY'S DATE** — MONTH DAY YEAR

15. **DAYTIME PHONE NUMBER** — ( ) AREA CODE

    DELIBERATELY FURNISHING (OR CAUSING TO BE FURNISHED) FALSE INFORMATION ON THIS APPLICATION IS A CRIME PUNISHABLE BY FINE OR IMPRISONMENT, OR BOTH.

16. **YOUR SIGNATURE**

17. **YOUR RELATIONSHIP TO THE PERSON IN ITEM 1 IS:**
    ☐ Self ☐ Natural Or Adoptive Parent ☐ Legal Guardian ☐ Other (Specify)

DO NOT WRITE BELOW THIS LINE (FOR SSA USE ONLY)

NPN	DOC	NTI	CAN	ITV
PBC	EVI	EVA	EVC	NWR	DNR	UNIT

EVIDENCE SUBMITTED

SIGNATURE AND TITLE OF EMPLOYEE(S) REVIEWING EVIDENCE AND/OR CONDUCTING INTERVIEW

DATE

DCL — DATE

Form **SS-5** (5/88) 1/85, 8/85, and 11/86 editions may be used until supply is exhausted

---

1. Your card will show your full first, middle, and last names <u>unless you show otherwise.</u> If you have ever used another name, show it on the third line. You can show more than one name on this line. Do not show a nickname unless you have used it for work or business.

2. Show the address where you want your card mailed. If you do not usually get mail at this address, please show an "in care of address," for example, c/o John Doe, 1 Elm Street, Anytown, State 00000.

3. If you check "other" under Citizenship, please attach a statement that explains your situation and why you need a Social Security number.

5. You do not have to answer our question about race/ethnic background. We can issue you a Social Security card without this information. However, this information is important. We use it to study and report on how Social Security programs affect different people in our nation. Of course, we use it only for statistical reports and do not reveal the identities of individuals.

13. If the date of birth you show in item 6 is different from the date of birth you used on an earlier application, show the date of birth you used on the earlier application on this line.

Do You Have the Legal Right to Work?

Anyone who works in the United States must be a citizen of this country or must provide documents that say he or she has the legal right to work in this country. If you are not a citizen, be sure to take the documents you need when you meet with an employer. All employers are required by law to check that noncitizens have the legal right to work. If you need such a document, contact the Immigration and Naturalization Service (INS).

POINTS TO REMEMBER

In this section, you learned that there are many ways of finding out what kinds of jobs are right for you. Some of the most important include:

- learning about your interests and work values so you can figure out what's important to you
- knowing your talents, skills, education, and training so you can use them to qualify for jobs
- reviewing your past work experience so your job search is easier
- understanding that jobs usually focus on one of the following four work tasks: data, ideas, people, objects

■ TAKING ✓ STOCK ■

WORKING VOCABULARY

Rewrite each sentence on a separate sheet of paper. Fill in the blanks with the correct word or words from the list below.

Note: There are more words than definitions.

background skills   **skill**
basic skills   **strengths**
data   **talents**
interests   **technical skills**
qualifications   **work values**

1. Employers expect you to have _____ _____, such as reading, writing, and doing math before they hire you.

2. Tasks that you learn easily are _____.

3. _____ _____ are skills that you use in many areas of your life.

4. Your skills can be counted as _____ for jobs.

5. Your _____ are the activities that you enjoy.

Getting Ready for Work 11

SKILLS FOR WORK

Suppose you want to begin job hunting. Before you do, make a list of all the things you could use as qualifications.

1. _____
2. _____
3. _____
4. _____
5. _____

YOU DECIDE

Suppose you could have a job doing all the things you enjoy in a workplace that you would like. On the lines below, describe the job and the surroundings. Then explain why you would like it.

_____
_____
_____
_____
_____

Can you think of any "real" jobs similar to this one?

_____

If so, what are they?

_____

FINDING OUT MORE

Choose a job that might interest you from the chart on page 8. Get a career resource book from your program coordinator. Then answer the following questions.

1. What job did you choose?

   _____

2. What are the qualifications for this job?

   _____
   _____

3. What are some of the duties performed?

   _____
   _____

4. What are the usual working hours?

   _____

5. What source did you use to find this information?

   _____

6. Do you still think you would like this job? _____ Why or why not?

   _____

SECTION TWO

FINDING A JOB LEAD

Rita filled the coffee cups. Then she sat at the kitchen table across from her sister Yolanda.

"I don't know," Rita said. "After eight years at home with the kids, it's hard to just go out and get a job."

"You're right," Yolanda replied. "But it's even harder to pay the rent and buy food and clothes these days."

"I know," Rita said. "That just makes it all the more necessary to find a job."

"Have you been looking?" Yolanda asked.

"Yes, I've been reading the help-wanted ads every day," Rita replied.

"There are other places to look besides the want ads," Yolanda said.

"Like where?" Rita asked.

"How about looking for postings on bulletin boards?" Yolanda asked.

"What do you mean?" Rita asked.

"I see all kinds of jobs posted on the bulletin board at the supermarket. And at the library and the community center," Yolanda replied. "You could see if there are any ads for companions or babysitters."

"I never thought of that," Rita said.

"And what about asking the neighbors? Or your friend Rosalie?

Isn't she a nurse? I'll bet she would know people who need a companion," Yolanda said.

"I never thought to ask her," Rita said. "But I'm sure she would help me."

Rita got up to refill their cups. "You better enjoy my coffee now, while you can," she said. "I'm going to be a busy working woman soon." ∎

There were many things that Rita had to think about in looking for a job. When you make a decision to join the work world, you should consider:

- how people can help you find a job
- where to look for help-wanted signs and how to respond to them
- how to read and use help-wanted ads
- how to read and use phone books
- how to present yourself in person and over the phone
- where you can go if you need special help
- how to find out about training programs

TALKING WITH PEOPLE YOU KNOW

Yolanda helped Rita to see that there are many places to look for jobs. But believe it or not, one of the best places to start is with your family, friends, and neighbors. These people may not be able to offer you a job, but they may know *other* people who can.

Many employers talk to their employees, clients, and suppliers when they have job openings. That's why people can sometimes tip you off to jobs that haven't been advertised.

You can start looking for work by telling your family and friends what kind of job you want. Then tell everyone you know—former employers, neighbors, and people in your community. The more people you tell, the more likely you are to find out about job openings.

People can also help you by describing different types of jobs they do. For example, Rita has a sister-in-law, Maria, who works as a salesclerk. If Rita were interested in working in sales, she might talk to Maria. Maria could describe her job and what she likes and dislikes about it.

 Putting the Word Out

Write the names of three people you would talk to if you were looking for a job. Then explain how each person might be able to help you. An example is done for you.

Name	How This Person Can Help
Tom	Got a job for his cousin at his company
1. _____	_____
2. _____	_____
3. _____	_____

ANSWERING HELP-WANTED SIGNS

You have probably seen signs in windows that say "Help Wanted." This is a common way that many restaurants, shops, and small businesses let people know that they have job openings.

Some employers advertise by placing **help-wanted** announcements on bulletin boards. The types of jobs that Rita was looking for are often posted on bulletin boards in:

- supermarkets
- shopping centers
- post offices
- community centers
- government buildings

You should read help-wanted signs carefully before you call or visit employers. If a sign includes a telephone number, write it down, then call. If there is no phone number, you can visit the employer.

However, if you drop in on an employer, be prepared for an **interview.** Be ready to answer questions about your education and job history. Be prepared to fill out an application form, too. You will read more about interviews and application forms in Sections 3, 4, and 5.

UNDERSTANDING HELP-WANTED ADS

One other place to look for jobs is in your local newspapers. Many employers place job ads in the **classified** (KLAS•uh•fyd) ad sections of newspapers.

New job ads appear in most papers every day. The Sunday papers usually carry the greatest number of ads.

Large papers have an **index** at the front that tells you what's in each section of the newspaper. The sections have letters (section A, section B, and so on) and page numbers. If the index says the classified ads begin on B3, you would turn to page 3 of section B. Small papers may use the last few pages for the classified ads.

The job listings are in the help-wanted category. They are in alphabetical order by job title.

Papers may list jobs under different titles, so you may need to look at the

Should You Drop In?

The way you present yourself when you meet an employer can help or hurt your chances of getting a job.

When you spot a help-wanted sign, you should ask yourself:

- Am I dressed well enough to go in and ask for a job?
- Can I remember enough personal information to fill out an application?
- Will I miss this chance if I wait?
- If I don't drop in now, when will I be able to return?

If you're not prepared to drop in, then come back as soon as possible. Otherwise the job might get filled.

Finding a Job Lead

entire help-wanted category. For example, one paper may list jobs for insurance clerks under the heading "Insurance," whereas another paper may list the same jobs under the heading "Clerk."

Employers often **abbreviate** (uh•BREE•vee•ayt), or shorten, words in their ads since they are paying for each line or letter. The chart on page 17 shows common abbreviations and their meanings. Refer to it when you need help in understanding abbreviations in an ad.

 ### What's in an Index?

The index below is an example of a front-page index in a large newspaper. Read it and answer the questions that follow.

INDEX			
National/International			Section A
Business			Section B
Metropolitan			Section C
Sports			Section D
Classified			Section E
Arts	B—15	Obituaries	D—29
Autos	E—22	Puzzles	C—26
Editorials	A—18	Real Estate	E—18
Help Wanted	E—1	Television	C—27

1. In which section of the newspaper could you find the classified ads?

   _____

2. On what page do the help-wanted ads begin? _____

3. Where might you find information on new businesses?

   _____

   In which section is that information?

   _____

4. Which categories are part of the classified section?

   _____

   _____

5. Look at a copy of your local newspaper. What is the name of the section in which the help-wanted ads are located?

   _____

BLIND ADS

Some help-wanted ads do not include the employer's name, address, or telephone number. These are called **blind ads** because you don't know who the employer is. How do you answer a blind ad? You would address a letter to a **box number** at the newspaper's address. This address may be listed on the front page of the classified section. If you can't find the address, call the newspaper and ask for the paper's address.

Some employers place blind ads because they don't want to receive phone calls. Others place them because they don't want their workers to know they have job openings. If you answer a blind ad, you may not hear from the employer. Employers who place these ads usually do not answer all the letters they receive.

ABBREVIATIONS IN HELP-WANTED ADS

The following chart can help you understand common abbreviations used in help-wanted classified ads.

Abbreviation	Meaning	Abbreviation	Meaning
apps.	applicants, applications	mo.	month
avail.	available	PT, pt	part-time
co.	company	pref.	prefer, preferred
exp.	experience	ref.	references
FT, ft	full-time	req.	require, required
HS, hs	high school	sal.	salary
hr.	hour	sec'y	secretary
immed.	immediate	tel.	telephone
K (as in $10K)	thousand	w/	with
M (as in $10M)	million	wk.	week, work
max.	maximum	wpm, w.p.m.	words per minute
min.	minimum	yr., yrs.	year, years
M-F	Monday through Friday		

Replying to Help-Wanted Ads

If you use the classified section in your job search, remember to:

- **Read the job ads early each day.** Apply right away for any job that interests you. If you wait too long, the job may get filled.
- **Look for the qualifications.** Some employers list many qualifications in their ads. If you have some of the qualifications, then apply for the job. Employers may hope to find the "perfect" person. But they often accept one who has some, but not all, of the qualifications.
- **Apply by phone.** If a job ad lists a telephone number but no address, call and ask how to apply for the job. Most employers will ask to meet with you before they make a decision to hire you.
- **Apply in person.** When an ad lists an address and says "Apply in person," go to that address. When you do, be prepared to meet with the employer. If the ad lists a time to show up, be on time.
- **Write to the employer.** Some ads list an address and tell applicants to write. In that case, you must send the employer a letter. (You will read more about these letters in Section 3.)
- **Read the ads carefully.** Avoid ads for jobs that say you must give money, buy sample products, or pay for training.
- **Keep a list of the ads you answer.** That way you can keep track of and follow up on employers who may not contact you right away.

What's in an Ad?

The blind ad below has many abbreviations in it. Write the ad out on the lines without using any abbreviations. Use the chart on page 17 if you need to. Then answer the questions that follow.

CLERICAL
Fast-growing co. needs FT clerical personnel w/1–3 yrs. office exp. Immed. openings. Send letter to: B1369 Austin Newspapers.

_____

_____

_____

_____

1. What type of job is being advertised?

   _____

2. Is the name of the company listed?

   _____

3. How would you answer this ad?

   _____

4. What experience are they asking for?

   _____

5. When is the job available?

   _____

USING OTHER SOURCES IN THE JOB HUNT

Another way to find a job is to call or write to companies that you want to work for. Your telephone book is a source that can help you do that. Most telephone books have two sections, white pages and yellow pages. In large cities the yellow pages may be bound in a separate book.

The white pages lists the names of people, businesses, and organizations in alphabetical order, along with their telephone numbers. The listings may include street addresses, too. You would use the white pages to look up the phone number of a company if you already knew the company's name.

The yellow pages lists companies, stores, and businesses along with their telephone numbers and addresses. It is divided into general business categories, such as "Physicians," "Restaurants," and "Insurance."

When you call a large company, ask for the **personnel** (purs•un•EL) **department.** If you're calling a small company or if the company doesn't have a personnel department, ask for the department or person that does the hiring.

Ask if the company has any job openings. If there are job openings, ask when you can visit the company to fill out a job application form. If there aren't any job openings, ask if the company has any apprenticeship programs. **Apprentices** (uh•PRENT•us•iz) earn wages as they learn a trade.

Using the Yellow Pages

When you use the yellow pages to look for a job, be as specific as possible.

For example, Betty is a manicurist. She looks in the yellow pages and sees three categories:

> BEAUTY SCHOOLS
> BEAUTY SHOPS
> BEAUTY SUPPLIES

While all three categories concern beauty, Betty should look under BEAUTY SHOPS since that is where a manicurist is most likely to be employed.

After each number below, there is a type of work experience. Following each type of experience are three categories that could be found in the yellow pages. Read the categories and choose the one that would most likely employ workers with that specific type of work experience.

1. Experience: fixing cars
   AUTOMOBILE SALES
   AUTOMOBILE REPAIRS
   AUTOMOBILE LEASING AGENTS

   Category: _____

2. Experience: taking care of children
   CHILD CARE—SUPPORT
      GROUPS
   CHILD CARE—CHILD CARE
      CENTERS
   CHILD CARE—REFERRAL
      AGENCIES

   Category: _____

3. Experience: building superintendent
   REAL ESTATE—MANAGEMENT
      COMPANIES
   REAL ESTATE—SALES
   REAL ESTATE—DEVELOPERS

   Category: _____

4. Experience: salesclerk
   RETAIL MARKETING—
      SALES
   RETAIL—STORES
   RETAIL—DISTRIBUTORS

   Category: _____

5. Write one type of work experience that you have. Then use your yellow pages to find the best category to look in.
   Experience:

   _____

   Yellow pages:

   _____

USING THE TELEPHONE

The way you present yourself over the phone can help you get a job. When you call about job openings, remember to:

- **Call from a quiet, private place.** You don't want to be interrupted.
- **Say who you are.** State your first and last name and the reason for your call. If you have permission to use someone's name, mention the name right away. For example, "This is Stan Williams. Greg Howell said I should call you. He said you might have an opening in your shipping department." Then ask questions.
- **Ask for the correct person.** In a small business, ask to speak to

Finding a Job Lead

the manager. In a large company, ask for the personnel department.

- **Speak clearly.** Be sure the other person can hear you. Talk slowly. Speak carefully and correctly.
- **Be polite.** Speak in a friendly tone. Thank anyone who helps you, even if there are no jobs available.
- **Ask if the employer wants to meet with you.** If you make an appointment, write down the time and date. Repeat it to the person who gave you the information to be sure it is correct.
- **Ask important questions.** Before you express your interest in a job, ask about certain details, such as hours, duties, and location. This is especially important if you won't be meeting with the employer.
- **Get people's names.** Write down the names of people you talk to, in case you need to call them again. Be sure you can spell and pronounce their names correctly.

   Calling an Employer

You are calling an employer to ask about an opening for a cashier's job. You saw the ad in the newspaper. Only the phone number was listed. The ad said, "Call and ask for Jim."

Act out this situation with another person. One takes the role of the job hunter. The other takes the role of the employer.

Before you begin, take a few minutes to prepare your role and think about some questions you might ask. After you play one role, switch with the other person and try the other role. Then answer the following questions.

1. How did you feel in the role of job hunter?
   _____

2. What do you feel you did well?
   _____
   _____

3. What do you need to improve?
   _____
   _____

4. How could you make that improvement?
   _____

5. What advice would you give to your role-play partner who acted as a job hunter?
   _____
   _____

CONTACTING STATE EMPLOYMENT SERVICES

It's a good idea to ask your state employment office for a list of jobs in your area. It may also have information about training programs.

You don't have to pay for the services offered by a state employment office. The state employment office provides help for all job hunters. It offers special help for people who have trouble finding work because they didn't finish high school or because they speak little or no English.

You can find the address and phone number of your state employment office by looking in your phone book under the name of your state. Some state employment offices may be called the "Job Service." If your phone book has blue pages that list government offices, you will find the number there.

If you visit the state employment office, you will have to fill out a form about your work history and skills. Be prepared to fill out the form by bringing information about your past schooling and work history. A counselor will read the completed form and then offer you advice on finding a job.

POINTS TO REMEMBER

In this section, you learned about the many ways of finding jobs. Some of the most important include:

- talking with family, friends, neighbors, and acquaintances
- responding to help-wanted signs
- answering help-wanted ads
- using the telephone book to find possible employers

■ TAKING ✓ STOCK ■

WORKING VOCABULARY

Use the clues to fill in the crossword puzzle with the correct word or words from the list below. Note: There are more words than definitions.

abbreviate   blind ad
apprentice   box number

classified   interview
help-wanted   personnel
index

ACROSS:
2. Where you reply to a blind ad
3. This tells what is in each section of the newspaper
6. To shorten words
7. A certain type of worker who learns a trade while earning wages

DOWN:
1. This department does the hiring in large companies
2. A help-wanted ad that doesn't include the employer's name, address, or telephone number
4. A meeting with an employer
5. The section of the newspaper in which job ads are placed

Finding a Job Lead   21

SKILLS FOR WORK

You are ready to begin job hunting. Make a list of five ways you would look for a job.

1. _____
2. _____
3. _____
4. _____
5. _____

YOU DECIDE

You are out to dinner one evening with a friend when you see a help-wanted sign in the restaurant. You have been looking for that type of job for weeks. Would you ask about the job? Or would you return later? Explain your answer.

_____
_____
_____
_____

FINDING OUT MORE

List two jobs that interest you. Write them on the lines that follow.

Go to two sources of employment that you learned about in this section to try to find a job opening. You could talk to people you know, look for help-wanted signs or ads, or read local phone books.

In the space below each job title, list the two sources and what you found. If, for example, you found an ad for that job in the classified section, list "help-wanted ad" as the source and then write the ad on the lines.

Job #1: _____

First source: _____

What you found there: _____
_____
_____

Second source: _____

What you found there: _____
_____
_____

Job #2: _____

First source: _____

What you found there: _____
_____
_____

Second source: _____

What you found there: _____
_____
_____

SECTION THREE

APPLYING YOURSELF

Lee was getting frustrated looking at the help-wanted ads. He had been looking for a job in food service for six weeks.

Most of the jobs he had seen required more experience than he had. But this morning he found one that sounded good. The only problem was that he didn't understand part of the ad. It just said, "Send an application letter to Box T2587."

"What does that mean?" Lee wondered. "Where is Box T2587?"

Lee called his Uncle Tao and asked him about the ad.

"The box number in the ad is at the newspaper's office," Uncle Tao explained. "Look on the first page of the want ads for the address."

Lee checked the first page and found the address for the box numbers. "You were right," Lee said. "Now can you tell me what to put in my application letter?"

"You should explain where you found out about the job and why you want it. You should also mention any experience you have that relates to the job."

"Like the summer job I had at the restaurant?" Lee asked.

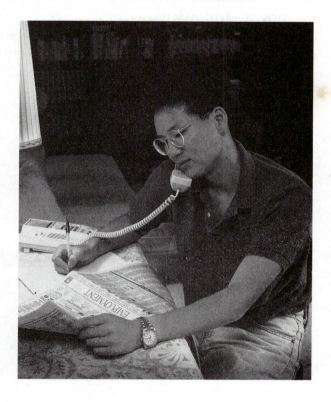

"Yes," Uncle Tao said. "But don't start the letter that way. First, you should say which job ad you're answering. And then you should say why you're interested in that job. After that, describe your skills and experience."

"OK," Lee said. "Thanks for all your help."

"No problem," Uncle Tao said. "In fact, if you want me to, I'll stop by tonight and check over your letter." ■

Applying Yourself

Lee had to think about several things when he looked for a job. When you begin your job search, you might need to know:

- how to apply for a job in person
- other ways by which you can contact employers
- how to fill out application forms
- how to write an application letter and a resume
- how to follow up on interviews

APPLYING IN PERSON

As you learned, many people seek jobs by looking for help-wanted signs in windows or on bulletin boards. When they do that, they usually apply for those jobs in person.

There are many good reasons to look for a job this way. You can see the actual workplace and what workers are doing. You get to fill out application forms. And you gain experience in meeting with employers, talking about jobs, and describing your strengths. Each time you do this, you become more comfortable.

MAKING NOTES FOR APPLICATION FORMS

You will find it a lot easier to fill out an application form if you carry a page of notes with you when you apply for a job. Those notes will help you fill in many details, such as:

- **Your Social Security number.**
- **The names and addresses of schools you attended and the dates**

Dropping In

Applying for jobs in person can be a very effective way of getting a job, if you know how to do it. You learned how to decide whether you were prepared enough to drop in on an employer in Section 2. Now let's look at what to do when you actually drop in.

- Don't drop in unless you are dressed for an interview.
- Introduce yourself and say why you're there. Look the other person in the eye. Shake hands firmly, if the other person holds out a hand.
- If the employer doesn't have time to talk to you, try to set up an appointment.
- Be enthusiastic, polite, and confident. Try to show that you're interested in the job. And that you feel you're qualified to do the work.
- Be prepared to fill out an application form. See the feature on this page for information on how to prepare ahead of time.
- If you're interviewed, ask questions about the job and the company. This shows that you care about the job.
- Before you leave, thank the interviewer or the person who took your application. Ask when a decision will be made about the job.
- Send a thank-you note to the interviewer.

when you attended them. Also, list any special courses you took.
- **The names, addresses, and telephone numbers of your last three employers.** Also, include your supervisors' names and the dates when you started and left.
- **The starting pay for your last three jobs.** Also, include how much you were paid at the time you left.
- **The names, addresses, and telephone numbers of three people who would recommend you for a job.** These **references** can include past employers or people who know your skills and abilities, such as teachers, coaches, or clergy members. Before you list people as references, get their permission. Find out what the reference will say about you. Also, make sure the phone numbers and addresses you have for them are up to date.
- **Your visa number and the date it expires.** You will need this only if you're not a citizen of the United States.

Choosing Your References

In the blank spaces that follow, write the names of two people you would ask to be references for you. List each one's current phone number and address. Then talk to each person and ask for his or her agreement to serve as a reference for you.

1. Name: _____

   Phone number: _____

   Address: _____

   Did this person give you permission to list him or her as a reference? _____

   If not, why not? _____

   _____

2. Name: _____

   Phone number: _____

   Address: _____

   Did this person give you permission to list him or her as a reference? _____

   If not, why not? _____

   _____

HOW TO FILL OUT JOB APPLICATION FORMS

When you visit an employer, you may be given an application form to complete. The form may be one or two pages long. All application forms serve the same purpose. They provide a way for employers to get information about applicants' backgrounds and qualifications.

Employers often use these forms to make hiring decisions, so fill them out *neatly*, *correctly*, and *completely*. Follow these steps when you fill out an application form:

- **Before you begin writing, look over the form.** Carefully read the instructions. Notice where to put different information. This will help

Applying Yourself

you avoid mistakes that can make the form look messy. If you don't understand the instructions, ask questions. Follow the directions that the instructions give.

- **Use a pen with black or dark blue ink.** Don't use a pencil. Unless you are told otherwise, print your answers. Write slowly and carefully. If the employer can't read your writing, your application may be thrown away.
- **Write your proper name on the application form.** Don't write your nickname.
- **Answer all of the questions on the form.** If a question doesn't apply to you, write the letters *NA* (for "not applicable") in that space. This shows that you haven't missed any questions. You may also use *NA* if there are certain personal questions on the form that you feel invade your privacy. Those questions concern age, race, marital status, religion, nationality, or physical or mental handicaps.
- **Answer all questions truthfully.** Employers usually call references, past employers, and schools to check the information on application forms. If the employer finds out that you provided false information, you won't get the job.
- **If you were found guilty of a crime, answer truthfully.** Employers often include a question about criminal **convictions** on applications. If you were convicted of a serious crime, be prepared to tell an interviewer about it.
- **Read over the completed form before you turn it in.** Be sure that you have answered all the questions. Check for misspellings and other errors. Make any corrections as neatly as possible.
- **Sign the application form.** Do this only after you have read all the fine print. When you sign a form, you are pledging that the information you have written is correct.

An Application Form to Fill Out

Choose one of the nine jobs from the chart on page 8 in Section 1. You are applying for that job in person. You have been handed the job application form on page 27 to fill out.

Complete it using real information about your background. You can fill in the shaded sections with information you have made up about the job.

In the future, you can use the background information on this form as your notes for filling out job application forms.

APPLYING BY LETTER

When Lee found the help-wanted ad for the food service job, he was confused. He had never answered an ad that asked him to send an **application letter.**

Many people apply for jobs by letter. Some of them respond to an ad as Lee did. Others may write to a specific company because they have heard of job openings.

APPLICATION FOR EMPLOYMENT

NAME (LAST)	(FIRST)	(MIDDLE)	SOCIAL SECURITY NO.

PRESENT ADDRESS CITY STATE ZIP CODE	AREA CODE	TELEPHONE NO.

PERMANENT ADDRESS (IF DIFFERENT FROM ABOVE)	AREA CODE	TELEPHONE NO.

POSITION APPLIED FOR	DATE AVAILABLE	
SALARY OR WAGE DESIRED	WILL YOU RELOCATE?	REFERRED BY

ARE YOU A U.S. CITIZEN? YES___ NO___	IF NOT A U.S. CITIZEN, LIST VISA NUMBER AND EXPIRATION DATE NUMBER_____ DATE_____

WITHIN THE LAST 5 YEARS HAVE YOU BEEN CONVICTED OF A FELONY?	☐ YES IF YES, GIVE DETAILS ON ☐ NO BACK PAGE	HAVE YOU EVER BEEN EMPLOYED BY OUR COMPANY? IF YES, GIVE DETAILS ON BACK PAGE	☐ YES ☐ NO

EDUCATION	INSTITUTION NAME AND ADDRESS	DID YOU GRADUATE?	MAJOR FIELD OF STUDY	CLASS STANDING
HIGH SCHOOL				
COLLEGE OR UNIVERSITY				
GRADUATE STUDY				
OTHER				

EMPLOYMENT RECORD	PLEASE LIST ALL EMPLOYMENT STARTING WITH MOST RECENT. ACCOUNT FOR ALL PERIODS (INCLUDING U.S. ARMED FORCES, PERIODS OF UNEMPLOYMENT, AND VOLUNTARY SERVICES).

LIST YOUR MOST RECENT POSITION HELD	MAY WE CONTACT YOUR PRESENT EMPLOYER? ☐ YES ☐ NO

EMPLOYER'S NAME AND COMPLETE ADDRESS/PHONE	DATES EMPLOYED		POSITION TITLE
	FROM	TO	NAME AND TITLE OF SUPERVISOR
	SALARY		
	START	FINAL	REASON FOR LEAVING

EMPLOYER'S NAME AND COMPLETE ADDRESS/PHONE	DATES EMPLOYED		POSITION TITLE
	FROM	TO	NAME AND TITLE OF SUPERVISOR
	SALARY		
	START	FINAL	REASON FOR LEAVING

EMPLOYER'S NAME AND COMPLETE ADDRESS/PHONE	DATES EMPLOYED		POSITION TITLE
	FROM	TO	NAME AND TITLE OF SUPERVISOR
	SALARY		
	START	FINAL	REASON FOR LEAVING

Applying Yourself

Employers ask for letters for many reasons. They may want to review an applicant's qualifications before taking the time to meet. Sometimes employers ask for letters because they know that an applicant who takes the time to write a letter is interested. Other employers may want a letter so they can judge each applicant's writing skills. This is true especially for jobs that involve writing.

The purpose of an application letter is to persuade an employer to set up an interview and consider you for a job. You can write an effective letter by following these steps:

- **Send the letter to a specific person, if possible.** Some help-wanted ads give the name of the person to whom you should write. If you don't have a specific name, you can call the company and ask who to send the letter to. If you can't get a specific person's name, address your letter to the personnel department.
- **Use a formal greeting.** A **greeting** is a line that introduces the letter. If you are writing to Jonas Robinson, the greeting should say, "Dear Mr. Robinson." If you don't know the person's name, use "Dear Sir or Madam" as the greeting.
- **Start the letter by telling the employer why you're writing.** In the first paragraph, say which job

When you write to employers, don't stretch your qualifications. If you do, you may be expected to perform tasks you aren't trained for.

you're interested in. Then tell why you want the job.
- **Tell the employer why you're qualified for the job.** In the second paragraph, write about your most important work experience, education, and other qualifications. Describe any special skills you have that would help you perform the job well. Don't stretch your qualifications.
- **Use formal English.** Don't use **slang**—it's too informal for an application letter. If you're not sure of how to spell a word, look it up in a dictionary.
- **In the last paragraph, ask the employer for a chance to meet.** Say when and where the employer can call or write you.
- **Check your letter carefully before you mail it.** If possible, ask someone else to proofread it. Another person may see errors that you missed. An employer may reject you if there are errors in your letter.

HOW TO WRITE AN APPLICATION LETTER

The way an application letter looks is just as important as what it says. If you follow the tips on page 30 when you write an application letter, you will increase your chances of getting an interview.

After reading the tips on writing an application letter, you will find tips on addressing a business envelope on page 31. The neatness and accuracy of the envelope is extremely important. After addressing the envelope and enclosing the letter, be sure to seal the envelope and put the correct postage on it.

An Application Letter to Write

In a newspaper, find a help-wanted ad for a job that you would like to apply for. Look for one that asks for a letter of application. If you don't find one, prepare an application letter for any job that you think you might like.

On a separate piece of paper, write the letter. Use the telephone book to find the address of the company if only the name and phone number are given in the ad. After you write the letter, answer these questions:

_____ Have I used an appropriate greeting?

_____ Have I explained which job I'm seeking and why I want the job?

_____ Have I written about my most important qualifications for the job?

_____ Have I described any special skills that I have?

_____ Have I used formal English throughout the letter?

_____ Have I asked for a chance to meet with the employer?

_____ Have I said when and where I can be reached?

_____ Is the letter neat and free of errors?

_____ Have I signed the letter?

Applying Yourself 29

GUIDELINES FOR WRITING APPLICATION LETTERS

```
                                            ①
                                        400 Mountain Road
                                        Cross Hills, FL 33123
                                        July 1, 199X
                                            ②

③  Mr. James Rossi, Director
   Route 23 Health Club
   2750 Route 23
   Cross Hills, FL 33224
                ④
⑤  Dear Mr. Rossi:

   I would like to apply for the position of lifeguard that you
   advertised in today's Daily News.
                ⑥
   I have recently graduated from Cross Hills High School, where
   I was a member of the swim team.  I have worked part time for
   the past two summers as a lifeguard at the Cross Hills Country
   Club. I have recently become a member of the Cross Hills
   Volunteer Ambulance Squad.
                ⑥
   I have Red Cross certification in both Advanced First Aid and
   Lifesaving.  In the fall I will be taking evening courses to
   become certified as an emergency medical technician.
                ⑥
   My schedule is flexible.  I am willing to work days, evenings,
   and weekends.
                ⑥
   I would like to meet with you to discuss my qualifications for
   this job.  You can contact me at 555-1256, or, if there is no
   answer there, you can leave a message with my sister at 555-
   5791.
                        ⑦ Sincerely,

                        Katherine O'Neill  ⑨

                        ⑧ Katherine O'Neill
```

Use plain, white, 8-1/2 by 11-inch bond paper and write on only one side.

Type the letter single spaced.

Leave a one-inch margin on the right and left and at the top and bottom of each page.

① Type your address in the upper right corner. Use one line for your street address and the next line for your city, state, and zip code.

② Type the date under the address.

③ Leave two blank lines after the date. Then, on the left side, type the employer's name and business address. Use one line for the person's name and title (or personnel department), the next line for the company name, the next line for the street address, and the next line for the city, state, and zip code.

④ Skip two lines after the employer's address.

⑤ Then, at the left side, type the greeting.

⑥ Within the main part of the letter, skip a line after each paragraph.

⑦ After the main part of the letter, skip a line and type the **closing.** This is the word or phrase that ends the letter. Closings to use in a business letter include "Sincerely," "Sincerely yours," and "Truly yours." The closing should line up with your address and date.

⑧ Skip four lines after the closing, then type your name so that it lines up with the closing.

⑨ Between the closing and your typed name, neatly sign your name.

30   Section Three

①

② Katherine O'Neill
400 Mountain Road
Cross Hills, FL 33123

③ Mr. James Rossi, Director
Route 23 Health Club
2750 Route 23
Cross Hills, FL 33224

① Use a standard white business envelope, 4 inches by 9 1/2 inches.

② Type your name and address in the upper left-hand corner of the envelope.

③ Type the employer's name and address in the center of the envelope.

WRITING A RESUME

There may be a few times during your job search when an employer will ask you for a **resume** (REZ•uh•may). This is a detailed, written summary of your background and qualifications.

As a rule, you don't need to provide a resume unless an employer asks for one. That's because many jobs don't require resumes. You probably won't need one if you're looking for an entry-level job or a job in mechanical trades, such as auto repair.

A resume is used to get an employer to consider you for a job. Your resume should tell the employer what kind of job you want, what kind of work you have done, and what schools you have attended. Resumes should be one page long if possible. They should contain more information than application letters do.

When you need to prepare a resume, use the following tips. As you read each item below, look at the sample resume on page 32.

- **Name, address, and telephone number.** If necessary, you may include both your temporary and your permanent addresses and phone numbers here. However, most people only list their current phone number and address.
- **Objective.** The **objective** should be a brief statement that describes the kind of job you're looking for.
- **Work experience.** Start this section with a heading such as "Work Experience" or "Experience." Begin the list with your current or most recent job. Limit your list to the

SETTING UP YOUR RESUME

Type your resume or have someone type it for you.

Use plain, white, 8-1/2 by 11 inch paper. Try to limit it to a single page. If necessary, you can use two pages.

Leave a one-inch margin on the right and left and at the top and bottom of each page.

Use capital letters and underlining to make important items stand out. That way, the employer can see the most important information right away.

① Type your name, address, and telephone number at the top. This information can go either on the left or in the center.

② Skip two lines. Then type your objective.

③ Skip two lines. Then type the next heading (Work Experience or Education).

④ Skip a line between each job or school under the heading.

⑤ Skip two lines. Then type your second heading (Work Experience or Education).

⑥ Skip a line between each item under the heading.

Use incomplete sentences throughout the resume. This will help you keep your resume short. For example, instead of saying, "My duties included typing letters, filing, and answering telephones," you can say, "Duties included . . ." or "Typed letters, filed . . ."

Check your resume carefully before you send it out. Ask someone else to read it. Another person might find mistakes that you missed. If you need to send copies of your resume to several employers, get photocopies made. You can have this done at any copying store.

```
                    Frank Ramirez
①                   1212 Northern Highway
                    Albuquerque, NM 87107
                    Telephone:  (505) 555-4920


②   Objective:           Position as Bank Teller


③   Work Experience:     ④

    September 1988       Cashier, part time, Smith's Department
       to present        Store, Albuquerque.
                         Ring up sales, handle customer service,
                         stock shelves, keep track of inventory on
                         computer.

    Summer 1988          File clerk, Central Avenue Insurance
                         Dunston, NM.
                         Typed and filed insurance claims and
                         applications, answered phones.

⑤   Education:           Currently enrolled in evening program,
                         "Intermediate Computing," at Wilson
                     ⑥   School, Albuquerque.

                         Central High School, Albuquerque.
                         Graduated June 1990, B average. Courses
                         included business math, bookkeeping, and
                         computers. Member of computer club.
```

Section Three

most recent or most important jobs. If your work experience has been varied, focus on the jobs you've had that are most closely related to the job you want.

For each job, write:

- the employer's name, address, and telephone number
- the months and years when you started and left the job
- the position or positions you held

Arrange each job in your list the same way. Briefly describe the type of work you did at each job. Try to show which skills you used in the job. For example, if you worked as a cashier, you might list, "Checked out store merchandise, handled customers' requests and complaints, counted receipts." Use "action" words such as *managed*, *ran*, *led*, and so on.

If you don't have full-time work experience, list part-time and summer jobs, volunteer work you have done, as well as your role as a homemaker. Just be sure to explain if it wasn't full-time or paid work experience.

■ **Education.** Start this section with a heading, such as "Education" or "Education and Training." List the schools you have attended and the diplomas, degrees, or certificates you have received. Include information on special courses you took. Start your list with the most recent school you attended and work backward.

List each school on a separate line. Include the school's name and location, the years you attended the school, and the diploma, degree, or certificate you earned. Arrange each school in your list the same way.

If you don't have much work experience, you may want to put the education list before the work list on your resume.

Writing Your Resume

It's a good idea to have a resume on hand when you're looking for a job. You never know when an employer will ask you for one.

The first step in writing a resume is deciding what information to include. The questions below can help you decide what to put on your resume.

1. What personal information should I list at the top of my resume?

_____

_____

2. What is my objective?

_____

_____

3. Which jobs were most important?

_____

_____

4. What education and training should I list?

_____

_____

5. What other information about my background or qualifications do I want to include in my resume?

   _____

   _____

On a separate sheet of paper, write a rough copy of your resume. Use the questions you just answered and the information on your application form on page 27 to help you write it. The resume on page 32 can help you organize it.

FOLLOWING UP ON JOB INTERVIEWS

Send a thank-you note right after the interview. This will keep your name in the interviewer's mind and show your interest in the job.

If you haven't heard from an employer within two weeks after you apply for a job, call and ask if the job has been filled.

The follow-up call can help you because:

- It shows that you're still interested in the job.
- It shows that you are able to follow through.
- It may help you stand out from other applicants who failed to make follow-up calls.
- If you aren't offered the job, the person you call may give you the name of a person to contact in another department or company.

When you make a follow-up call, say that you're still interested in the position. Try to find out the date when the employer plans to make a hiring decision.

Making follow-up calls will be easier if you keep good records of your job search. Keep a notebook with a page for each employer you contact. Make notes about each application letter or resume you send, each application form you fill out, and each discussion you have with an employer. Write down the date and purpose of each contact and the name of the person you dealt with. Then write down how the contact ended.

Calling an Employer

You are calling an employer on the telephone to follow up on an application letter that you sent a week ago. You were replying to an ad that you saw in the newspaper.

Get together with another student to act out this situation. One person takes the role of the job hunter. The other takes the role of the employer.

Before you begin, take a few minutes to prepare your role and think about some questions you might ask.

After you play one role, switch and try the other. Then answer the following questions.

1. How did you feel as the job hunter?

   _____

   _____

2. What do you feel you did well?

   _____

   _____

3. What do you need to improve?

   _____

   _____

4. How could you make that improvement?

   _____

   _____

POINTS TO REMEMBER

In this section, you learned that there are many ways to make contact with employers. Some of the most important ways include:

- applying for jobs in person
- filling out job application forms
- writing and sending application letters
- writing and sending resumes
- following up on interviews with a thank-you letter and phone call

■ TAKING ✓ STOCK ■

WORKING VOCABULARY

On each blank after each definition, write the correct word or words from the list.

Note: There are more words than definitions.

application letter	**objective**
closing	**references**
conviction	**resume**
greeting	**slang**

1. These people recommend you for a job.

   _____

2. You begin a letter with this.

   _____

3. This informal language shouldn't be used in an application letter.

   _____

4. This statement describes the kind of job you want.

   _____

5. You put this at the end of a letter.

   _____

6. You give this detailed written summary to employers.

   _____

Now find each answer from 1–6 in the puzzle below and circle it. The words can be forward or backward.

```
e r a u b d a s g t
h v k l e m t o r o
r e f e r e n c e s
a n e p e w o i e t
d c l o s i n g t e
a u o t u o k n i s
w i l l m e m a n d
u t j e e q i l g o
b e z k o n s s e v
e v i t c e j b o w
```

Applying Yourself 35

SKILLS FOR WORK

You are going to apply for a job. You know that you will have to fill out an application form, and you want to make notes ahead of time so you're prepared. Make a list of the six pieces of information that you should have in your notes.

1. _____
2. _____
3. _____
4. _____
5. _____
6. _____

YOU DECIDE

You have called a previous supervisor to ask him to be a reference for you. The supervisor tells you that he would rather not be a reference for you. Would you ask him why? Would you use him as a reference anyway? Explain your answer.

_____
_____
_____
_____

FINDING OUT MORE

Use the help-wanted section of your local newspaper to find three ads for jobs that you are interested in.

On the lines below, write the job title and the way that the ads tell you to apply for the jobs.

Then answer the questions that follow.

Job title #1: _____

How to apply: _____

_____

Job title #2: _____

How to apply: _____

_____

Job title #3: _____

How to apply: _____

_____

How many of the three jobs asked applicants to apply in person? _____

How many of the three jobs asked applicants to send an application letter? _____

Were there any other ways to apply listed in your three ads? _____

If so, what were they? _____

_____
_____

Which way of applying was the most common in your three ads?

_____
_____

SECTION FOUR

Q & A: THE JOB INTERVIEW

"That outfit is perfect for an interview," Anne said.

"Sure, I'll look great," Cherise said. "But how will I *sound*? I've never been on a formal interview before."

"Hey, I have an idea," Anne said. "Why don't we practice? You be you, and I'll be the interviewer. I've been on lots of interviews, and I know what kinds of questions they ask."

"OK," Cherise said, smiling.

"Why do you want to work at Harvard Investments as a receptionist?" Anne asked in her new role.

"I want to work as a receptionist because I like meeting people," Cherise said. "And I've heard Harvard Investments is a great place to work."

"You know, in this job, you also have to handle the phones, take messages, type, and file," Anne said. "Do you think you can handle all that?"

"Oh, yes," Cherise said. "I'm very well organized. I'm a good typist. And I've taken classes to learn about general business skills like filing."

"Do you have any questions about the job?" Anne asked.

"I thought you were supposed to ask *me* the questions," Cherise said.

"Most interviewers ask applicants if they have questions," Anne said.

"What should I ask?" Cherise said.

"Ask details about the job," Anne explained. "You might ask how much of the job involves typing."

"Thanks," Cherise said. "This has been a big help." ■

Q & A: The Job Interview   37

Cherise needed to consider many issues before going on her first interview. Likewise, when you prepare for an interview, you should:

- Write down key questions you want to ask.
- Practice your answers.
- Practice interviewing with a friend or relative.
- Be prepared to take tests.
- Take care of last-minute details and plan your time.

KNOWING WHAT TO EXPECT

Cherise was nervous about her job interview because she didn't know what to expect. She had never been on a formal job interview before.

After she practiced with her friend, she felt more confident. Anne helped her prepare for the interview. Anne asked her some questions so Cherise knew what to expect.

You can never know exactly what will happen on a job interview. But by practicing you can prepare yourself for many possible situations.

An employer who invites you for an interview usually feels that you are qualified for the job. Most employers interview only the best-qualified applicants for each opening. For this reason, you should feel confident before your interview. You've made it to the starting gate.

Employers usually look carefully at each applicant's **personal traits.** These are the qualities, such as a sense of humor, that make each person different. Employers look for certain personal traits in the people they hire. Those traits include having a positive attitude and listening well. You can show a positive attitude by being friendly and cheerful.

The applicant who makes the most favorable impression during an interview usually gets the job. How can you make a good impression during an interview? By being prepared and by having a positive attitude. Steps that you can follow to help you include finding out about the job, preparing to ask questions, and preparing to answer questions.

FINDING OUT ABOUT THE JOB

You can prepare for an interview by finding out as much as you can about similar jobs. This is especially helpful if you're applying for a specific job for the first time.

Look up the job in a career resource book. Two of the best books are the *Occupational Outlook Handbook* and the *Dictionary of Occupational Titles*. Either your program instructor or your coordinator has these books, or you can find them in the reference section of a public library.

By reading about specific jobs, you can learn what the main duties and primary work tasks are. For example, you would learn whether you would work mainly with data, ideas, people, or objects. You can then use the information that you find to help you relate your background to the particular job you're applying for.

The librarian in your local library can help you find information about jobs.

For instance, if you're applying for a job as a salesperson in a clothing store, you would look under the title "Retail Salesperson" in the *Dictionary of Occupational Titles* or the *Occupational Outlook Handbook*. You would read that these workers spend most of their time dealing with customers. If you had previous experience working with the public in any job, you could relate that background skill to the work that a salesperson does during your interview.

PREPARING QUESTIONS

Before an interview, use the information you have found at the library or in resource books to prepare questions. Make a list of these questions and take them with you on the interview. This will show your interest in the company and the job. You should ask the following kinds of questions:

- **Questions about the duties.** Ask what you would be expected to do and where you would do it. For example, for a job as a delivery person, you might ask how many deliveries you would make a day and in which neighborhoods you would make them.
- **Questions about the job opening.** If you don't already know the answers to the following questions, then you should ask:
  - when you would start
  - what hours you would work
  - whether you would work any overtime
  - what the fringe benefits are
- **Questions about the hiring decision.** Be sure to ask when the employer plans to make a decision. The interviewer may offer to contact you when a decision is made. If he or she doesn't, then ask if you can call on a certain day to find out about the employer's decision.

 Asking Questions About a Job

Imagine that you have applied for the job in the ad on page 40 and have been invited for an interview. Make a list of five questions you would like to ask during the interview. List the questions in the order that you would ask them.

> **FOOD SERVICE.** We are accepting applications for Line Server. Daytime hours only. Benefits incl. paid holidays, meals, medical insur., and uniforms. For more info, call 555–5250. Ask for Lori.

Questions to Ask in an Interview

1. _____
2. _____
3. _____
4. _____
5. _____

QUESTIONS YOU CAN EXPECT

When you go on an interview, be prepared to answer many questions about yourself and your qualifications. Some of those questions may be simple ones that you can answer yes or no. For example, you may be asked if you have ever dealt with customers. You could answer yes, but a better answer would be: "Yes. I rang up customers' purchases and sometimes had to handle their exchanges and refunds."

You may also be asked more difficult questions or questions that require more detailed answers. Your answers to those questions may determine whether you get the job. Bear in mind that interviewers value good communication skills, so the better you're able to express yourself, the better your chances of landing the job.

Before you go on an interview, think about how you would answer specific questions. You can't know exactly what the interviewer will ask. But if you think about the possibilities ahead of time, you will be prepared no matter what. Some common questions include:

- Why are you applying for this job?
- Why do you think you can do this job?
- What can you do for us?
- Why should I hire you?
- What are your strengths?
- What are your weaknesses?
- Did you like school? What was your best subject?
- Why did you leave school before you graduated?
- What did you like most (or least) about your last job?
- Why did you leave your last job? (Why do you want to leave the job you have now?)
- Have you ever been fired from a job? (If you say yes, be prepared to explain.)

The interviewer may also say, "Tell me something about yourself." This is a chance for you to spend a minute or two describing how your background and skills relate to the job you're interviewing for. The interviewer doesn't expect to hear about your personal life, such as your family or your favorite hobbies.

If you review the questions you answered in Section 1 on pages 2, 3, 4, and 5 and the resume you wrote for Section 3, you will be able to answer most of these questions. Review what you wrote about your interests, values, talents, skills, and work experience. Then think about how your background relates to the job. This can help you explain why you feel you're qualified for the job.

In addition, think about ways to describe how dependable you are. Give examples of your dependability. For instance, are you always on time or early to work? Did you have few or no absences last year? These details are very important to employers.

Answering Questions About a Job

Read the help-wanted ad you used on page 40. Once again, imagine that you are preparing for the interview. Practice by answering the following questions.

1. How dependable are you?

   _____

   _____

2. What are your strengths?

   _____

   _____

3. What are your weaknesses?

   _____

   _____

   _____

4. What did you like most about your last job?

   _____

   _____

   _____

   _____

5. What did you like least about your last job?

   _____

   _____

   _____

   _____

LISTENING AND WATCHING AS YOU PRACTICE

After you have thought about how you would answer questions during an interview, practice them aloud. Record your answers on a tape recorder and play them back. As you listen, ask yourself:

- Did I speak clearly?
- Did I sound friendly and enthusiastic?
- Did I sound like I knew what I was talking about?

If your speech is unclear, try speaking more slowly. Say each word carefully. If you didn't sound interested, keep practicing.

Try to rehearse in front of a mirror, too. As you talk, pay attention to your **body language.** Your body sends certain messages. Those messages are based on your facial expressions, the **gestures** (JES • cherz) you make with your hands, and your posture. For example, if you slouch in your chair and don't look the interviewer in the eye, you will send out a negative message.

Eye contact is extremely important in an interview. If you look the interviewer in the eye, you will come across as honest and sincere.

You also want to come across as friendly and interested in what the interviewer is saying. You can do that by sitting up straight and looking directly at the interviewer. In addition, sit still and really listen to what the interviewer is saying.

SHOWING A POSITIVE ATTITUDE

When some people see half a glass of water, they say the glass is half full. Others describe the glass as being half empty. People see the glass differently because of their attitude. People with a positive attitude see the glass as half full. People with a negative attitude see it as half empty.

The way you see things and the way you talk about them can make a big difference in an interview. Employers want workers who have a positive attitude about themselves and their work. You can learn how to express thoughts in a positive way.

The questions below are ones that you might be asked in an interview. After each question are two possible responses. One of the responses is better because it is stated in a more positive way. Compare the two answers so that you understand why one answer is better.

Question: Why are you applying for this job?

- Positive: Because I'm interested in working for your company.
- Negative: Because I don't like the job I have now.

Question: Why did you leave school before you graduated?

- Positive: I had to get a job so I could help support my family.
- Negative: It was a waste of time.

Question: Why do you want to leave the job you have now?

- Positive: I want a more challenging job.
- Negative: It's boring.

One question that often comes up in the interview is: How did you get along with your last supervisor? This can be a hard question, especially if the working relationship you had with your supervisor wasn't good. The important thing to keep in mind when answering a question like this is never to speak negatively about former employers.

Would any of your answers be negative? If so, try to answer them again in a more positive way.

HOW TO PRACTICE FOR INTERVIEWS

Sometimes it's easier to ask and answer questions if you can practice with a friend or relative. Anne helped Cherise prepare for her interview by doing this.

Anne played the part of the interviewer. She asked Cherise questions that a real interviewer might ask. Then Cherise learned why it's important to ask questions during an interview.

Anne could have helped Cherise even more by telling her what kind of impression she made. Did she stand, sit, and talk in a way that created a good impression? Did she speak clearly and intelligently?

If you don't have much experience interviewing, get some practice. Ask a friend or relative to play the role of the employer. Try to get someone who has been on job interviews and knows what they are like.

- Dress the same way you would for a real interview.
- Greet the other person just as you would greet an employer.
- Shake hands firmly.
- Smile and look the other person in the eye.
- Give the answers you would give to the employer.
- Use the same gestures and talk the same way you would in a real interview.
- Stand and sit straight.

Afterward, ask the other person what kind of impression you made. Were you dressed well enough? Did

Both of these people are going to an interview. Can you guess which one prepared and practiced ahead of time?

you give answers that would make an employer want to hire you? Were you friendly and enthusiastic? Did you come across as having a positive attitude? Ask the other person for suggestions on how you might make a better impression.

Taking Time to Practice

Practice interviewing with a friend, relative, or classmate. One person should play the role of the interviewer. The other should play the role of the applicant. Then switch roles, so that each of you gets a chance to play both parts.

When you are playing the part of the interviewer, ask questions such as those listed on page 40. Then fill out the following form to let the applicant know what kind of impression he or she made. Explain why the applicant made a good impression or how the applicant could have made a better one.

	Excellent	Good	Fair
Appearance	☐	☐	☐
Posture	☐	☐	☐
Speech	☐	☐	☐
Attitude	☐	☐	☐
Questions asked	☐	☐	☐
Answers to questions	☐	☐	☐
Overall impression	☐	☐	☐

Explanation _____

_____

_____

_____

When playing the part of the applicant, ask questions about duties, the job opening, and the hiring decision. Answer the interviewer's questions as positively as you can.

Then fill out the following form to rate your own performance during the interview. Explain why you think you made a good impression or how you could have made a better one.

	Excellent	Good	Fair
Appearance	☐	☐	☐
Posture	☐	☐	☐
Speech	☐	☐	☐
Attitude	☐	☐	☐
Questions asked	☐	☐	☐
Answers to questions	☐	☐	☐
Overall impression	☐	☐	☐

Explanation _____

_____

_____

PREPARING TO TAKE TESTS

At the interview, the employer may want to test your aptitude, skills, general abilities, or personal traits. Employers use these tests to learn which applicants are best suited to jobs.

If you get nervous about taking tests, remember that the purpose of tests is to help you. If you are well suited to the job, the test results will help show the employer that. If you don't do well on the test, then the job may not be right for you.

There are several types of tests that employers give:
- aptitude tests
- skill tests
- personality tests

An **aptitude test** measures your natural abilities for performing or learning certain kinds of tasks. An aptitude test may measure if you have the ability to do clerical tasks or work that involves numbers. Because aptitude tests measure your **potential** (pu•TEN•shul) to develop skills, you can't study for them.

Some aptitude tests involve writing

answers to questions. Others require you to perform simple tasks. For example, a test of your mechanical aptitude may include putting nuts and bolts together.

Employers may also give tests that measure your skill at doing specific tasks. For example, if you apply for a clerical job, such as secretary, word processor, file clerk, or bank teller, the employer may test your clerical skills. Depending on the job, you may be given a typing test or a test in filing, shorthand, or math.

Some employers give **personality tests,** or **adjustment tests.** These tests show whether you have the personal qualities that the job requires. For example, an employer may want to know whether you are talkative or quiet, how cooperative you are, if you are aggressive, and much more. Employers also use these tests to decide whether applicants will fit into the workplace and get along well with co-workers.

A FEW MORE DETAILS TO CONSIDER

Before the interview, there are a few last-minute details that you need to take care of.

- If you already have a job, and you need to take time off for an interview, arrange to do so as soon as possible. If you need to, arrange for someone else to take your shift or do your work that day.
- Schedule a babysitter, if you normally watch your children during the time of the interview. Have a backup babysitter or plan in case the babysitter cancels at the last minute.
- A day or two before the interview, pick out the clothes that you plan to wear. (We will discuss what to wear to an interview in Section 5.) Check to make sure that the clothes are clean and ironed. Make sure that your shoes are polished. You don't want to worry about these details the morning of the interview.
- Arrange for transportation to get to the interview. If you'll be driving, check the car. If you'll be taking public transportation, check the schedules in advance.
- If you are meeting an employer for the first time, be prepared to fill out an application form. That means that you should prepare your notes, as discussed on pages 24 and 25, ahead of time and put them with any other items you plan to take to the interview.

HOW TO PLAN YOUR TIME

Arriving on time for a job interview is essential. In fact, you should plan to arrive a few minutes early.

You can do this by figuring out how to get to the interview and how long it will take you to get there. If possible, make the trip before the interview, so you can be sure of the directions and how much time you need.

When you figure out your time, take into account traffic, especially if you'll be going at a different time of day. Be sure to leave time for walking to or from a bus stop or train station, finding a taxi, or parking your car.

Take into account how much time you will need to:

- Bathe and dress for the interview.
- Take a child to a babysitter or do other chores before you leave.
- Get to the interview a few minutes early, so you will feel relaxed instead of rushed.

If you have an emergency and you will be late for the interview or you have to cancel it, call the employer and explain. If possible, reschedule when you call.

POINTS TO REMEMBER

This section covered several points that you must think about when preparing for a job interview. The most important are:

- finding out about the job's tasks
- preparing ahead of time to ask questions
- practicing answering questions that interviewers frequently ask
- preparing to take employment tests
- checking to make sure small details are taken care of
- planning how much time you will need to get to the interview

■ TAKING ✓ STOCK ■

WORKING VOCABULARY

Rewrite each sentence on a separate sheet of paper. Fill in the blank with the correct word or words from the list below. Note: There are more words than definitions.

adjustment test **personality test**
aptitude test **personal traits**
body language **potential**
gestures

1. If you have the personal qualities for a job, a(n) _____ _____ and a(n) _____ _____ will show it.

2. When you practice for an interview in front of a mirror, watch your _____ .

3. Employers look at your individual qualities, or your _____ _____ , when they interview you.

4. If you can develop certain skills easily, then you have a high _____ for those skills.

SKILLS FOR WORK

A friend has asked you to help him practice for his first interview. As part of that practice, you have to help him make a list of questions to ask the interviewer. List five questions you would suggest he ask.

1. _____
2. _____
3. _____
4. _____
5. _____

YOU DECIDE

You have an interview for a job that you're very interested in. Your interview is scheduled for 10 A.M. tomorrow, but you can't find a babysitter to watch your children. On the lines below, explain what you would do.

_____
_____
_____
_____

FINDING OUT MORE

Choose a job that you would like to have. Then use the *Occupational Outlook Handbook* or the *Dictionary of Occupational Titles* to answer the following questions.

1. What is the job title?

_____

2. What source did you use?

_____

3. What are the main duties?

_____
_____
_____

4. What are the primary work tasks?

_____
_____
_____

5. How could you relate your background to this job?

_____
_____
_____

Q & A: The Job Interview

SECTION FIVE
A WINNING INTERVIEW

"Hey, Pete. I'm back," Will Hoffman called as he took off his coat.

"I'm in here, Dad," Pete called from the living room. "How did the interview go?"

"I think it went well," Will said. "Mr. Arnold, the boss, was impressed with my experience as a mechanic."

"So he liked you?" Pete asked.

"I think so," Will replied. "But he wanted to know why I didn't work for two years."

"What did you tell him?"

"I told him the truth. That I was sick. And that the doctor said I couldn't work because of my back."

"What did he say?" Pete asked.

"He wanted me to explain," Will said.

"But you're OK now," Pete said.

"Sure. But I had to convince Mr. Arnold of that," Will said. "Mechanics do hard work. Mr. Arnold doesn't want to hire someone who might get sick again."

"So you didn't get the job?"

"I didn't say that," Will said. "When I told Mr. Arnold that I've been back at work for three years and haven't had any trouble with my back, he sounded really interested."

"So you got the job?" Pete asked.

"I'll find out tomorrow," Will replied. "Mr. Arnold said he would check my references and call me tomorrow."

"Good job, Dad," Pete said. ■

During his job interview, Will had to think about many things. When you go on a job interview, you should:

- try to make a lasting impression
- be ready to answer difficult questions
- know about your legal rights
- know how to end the interview
- follow up after the interview

MAKING A LASTING IMPRESSION

Will Hoffman made a good impression during his job interview with Mr. Arnold for many reasons. For one, he had a positive attitude about himself and his work. He also expressed himself well and answered Mr. Arnold's questions clearly, completely, and honestly. In addition, he asked questions about the job duties and the company and showed his interest in the job.

When you have a job interview, you want to make a lasting impression as Will did. You can do that by preparing yourself and by working on your appearance and your behavior.

How you look is very important in a job interview. Interviewers will immediately notice the way you dress and groom yourself. They will form an opinion of you based on your cleanliness or **hygiene** (HY•jeen), your clothing, and your grooming. For example, if you wear wrinkled clothes and arrive with your hair uncombed, people may think you don't care about your appearance. They may think you have the same attitude about your work.

When you dress for an interview, make sure your clothes are clean, pressed, and in good repair. A man applying for an office or sales job should wear a suit or sports jacket and tie. A woman should wear a dress, suit, or skirt and blouse. If you're applying for a job that involves **manual labor,** or using your hands as part of your job, you can dress more casually. You should still look neat and clean.

Your hygiene and grooming are as important as your clothing when you want to make a good impression. See the feature on page 50 for hygiene and grooming tips.

Your behavior will affect the impression you make, too. Interviewers will watch the way you act. You will impress them more if you're enthusiastic, honest, and polite.

INTERVIEWING DO'S AND DON'TS

There are many do's and don'ts that you should be aware of before you go on an interview. They will help you make a good impression.

When you go on an interview, always go alone. If someone drives you, have him or her wait outside. Upon your arrival for an interview, give your name to the receptionist or secretary. You will probably have to wait a few minutes in an outer office before meeting the interviewer. You can use this time to see how the office is set up and observe what types of work people are doing.

When you meet the interviewer, shake hands firmly. You should take a seat only if it's offered. And remember never to smoke or chew gum during an interview. It is a good idea to let the interviewer control the interview, and never interrupt when the interviewer is talking. When it's your time to speak, use standard English. Don't use informal language or slang. And never curse or use **profanity** (pro•FAN•ut•ee). Be sure to answer all questions completely.

You should not criticize former employers or mention any personal problems that you may have. It's best to let the interviewer bring up the subject of money. If the interviewer doesn't, you can bring it up at the end of the interview.

Greeting an Interviewer

Imagine that you are meeting an employer for the first time. The employer's secretary called you last week to set up the interview. Now you are at the company, and the employer is standing in front of you waiting to greet you.

Act out this situation with one of your classmates. One person plays the part of the job hunter. The other plays the part of the employer. Before you begin, give your classmate your name.

After you play one part, switch and try the other. Then answer the following questions.

1. How did you feel as the job hunter?

   _____
   _____
   _____

Hygiene and Grooming Tips

Here are some hygiene and grooming tips that will help you make a good first impression on an interviewer:

- Brush your teeth and be sure your breath is fresh. It helps to have a mint before the interview.
- Bathe and use deodorant before you dress for the interview.
- Make sure your ears, hair, and fingernails are clean.
- Males should wear black, blue, or brown shoes that are clean, polished, and in good repair.
- If you're a woman, wear plain nylon stockings, without patterns. If you're a man, wear socks of a solid dark color, with no holes in them.
- If you polish your fingernails, be sure the polish is not chipped. Also, don't wear flashy colors.
- If you use cologne or makeup, use it lightly.
- Don't wear sunglasses, revealing clothing, or anything else that's flashy. If you do, you might not be taken seriously.

If you have to wait before an interview begins, observe the people and make a mental note of the work environment.

2. Did you look the interviewer in the eye and shake hands firmly?
   _____

3. What do you feel you did well?
   _____
   _____
   _____

4. What do you need to improve?
   _____
   _____
   _____

5. How could you make that improvement?
   _____
   _____
   _____

6. What advice would you give to your classmate in the role of job hunter?
   _____
   _____
   _____

A Winning Interview 51

ANSWERING DIFFICULT QUESTIONS

Some interviews are more trying than others. You may be asked questions that you have difficulty answering. Or you may have to discuss problems that you had in the past.

Interviews can be especially difficult if you have had problems that you are afraid will stand in the way of getting the job. In Will's case, for example, Mr. Arnold noticed that there was a two-year gap in Will's employment history. Mr. Arnold asked Will for an explanation.

Will handled the situation well. He was honest about the problem he had had with his back. And he explained that he had been well and working for the past three years.

If you've had problems in the past, such as gaps in employment or being treated for alcohol or drug abuse, think ahead of time about how you will explain them during the interview. If an interviewer asks you for an explanation, describe the situation honestly and explain how you resolved the problem. Thinking problems through before the interview will help you be prepared and will strengthen your confidence.

Many employers will hire qualified applicants who have had problems, if they show proof that they have recovered from an illness or learned from a past mistake. If you lie about a problem, however, the employer may learn the truth later and fire you for lying about your background.

A Difficult Question for You

You can prepare for difficult questions by thinking about how you would answer them ahead of time. On a separate sheet of paper, write a difficult question that you may have to answer. You can be honest—no one needs to read your response.

Think about how you would answer the question. Then on the same piece of paper, write what your answer would be.

AN APPLICANT'S RIGHTS

You have learned that you will be better prepared for an interview if you know what to expect. You also should know what should *not* happen during an interview.

Employers should not treat you differently because of your race, religion, national origin, ancestry, age, or sex. When employers do that, they're **discriminating** (dihs•KRIHM• uh•nayt•ing) against you.

Employers may not discriminate against workers with handicaps either, unless the handicaps make them unable to do the work. There are federal and state laws that protect people from discrimination.

Although there are laws to protect you against discrimination, it's still possible that an interviewer will ask for information that could be used to discriminate against you. If you're asked such a question, keep in mind that if you answer it, the employer may discriminate against you. However, if you refuse to answer the question, the employer may not hire you. Either way, however, there is something you can do.

If you feel you were not hired because of discrimination, you can contact the nearest office of the federal **Equal Employment Opportunity Commission** (EEOC). This agency enforces federal **civil rights** laws. Your civil rights are also sometimes called your **constitutional** (kahn•stu•TOO•shun•ul) rights. Those are the rights that are granted to every U.S. citizen by the U.S. Constitution.

In addition, you can contact your state's civil rights commission, which enforces state laws against discrimination. These agencies will listen to your side of the story and then will listen to the employer's side. If the agency finds that the employer broke the law, you may get the job or receive some form of payment for damages.

If you believe an employer has discriminated against you, you can also get help from private organizations. One such group is the American Civil Liberties Union (ACLU). Lawyers from this organization will represent people who claim they have been discriminated against and denied their civil rights.

HOW TO END THE INTERVIEW

The way that you end an interview can leave a lasting impression. Be alert for signals that the interview is coming to an end.

An interviewer might signal the end by closing the folder that contains your application or by standing up. If he or she gives you one of these signals, briefly ask your

---

Questions You Don't Have to Answer

During an interview, you may think that you have to answer every question you're asked. However, unless a question relates directly to the job you're seeking, an employer has no right to ask it. In fact, some questions may even *break* federal or local laws. An interviewer should not ask you any of the following questions:

■ How old are you?
■ Are you single or married?
■ Do you have children? Do you plan to have children?
■ Do you have child care arranged? What would you do if your child was sick on a workday?
■ Do you have any physical handicaps?
■ Of what race do you consider yourself to be?
■ What country were you born in?
■ Do you live by yourself?
■ Do you drink alcohol or use other drugs?

If an interviewer asks you any of these questions, or any other question that seems too personal, you have a right to refuse to answer. Or you could ask how the information relates to the job, then decide whether to answer the question.

final questions. Before you leave, try to get all of the information you need to make a decision about the job. If you haven't talked about salary or benefits yet, ask about them.

If an interviewer tells you at the end of the interview that you don't have the job, ask him or her on what information the decision was based. You could learn what you did wrong. Or you might learn that you didn't have the right qualifications for the job. Either way, this information can help you when you interview for other jobs in the future.

If the interviewer ends the interview by offering you the job, you may want to ask for some time—perhaps a day or two—to make a decision. However, if you're absolutely certain of your decision, you can accept or refuse the offer right away.

In most cases, a decision isn't made at the end of the interview. Some positions require more than one interview with more than one person before a job is filled. If the interviewer doesn't tell you when the hiring decision will be made, ask about it. Find out when a decision will be made and if you can call to learn the final decision.

At the end of every interview, thank the interviewer for his or her time. If you have already decided that you don't want the job, tell the interviewer. You don't have to explain your reasons unless asked.

On the other hand, if you're very interested in the job, say so. Then the interviewer will know where you stand.

How to Rate an Interview

After a job interview, you should rate your performance. If you do that, you can figure out what you did well and what you need to improve.

Use the questions below to help you rate interviews.

- Was I on time for the interview? If not, how could I have avoided being late?
- Did I tell the interviewer everything I wanted him or her to know about me? If not, what else should I have said?
- Did I say anything negative about myself? If so, how could I have avoided it?
- Did I find out everything I needed to know about the job? If not, what else should I have found out?
- Did the interviewer ask questions that I couldn't answer? If so, how can I be prepared next time?
- What kind of impression did I make? How might I have made a better impression?

HOW TO FOLLOW UP ON THE INTERVIEW

Right after the interview, send a brief letter to thank the interviewer for his or her time. Type the letter on plain 8 1/2- by-11-inch paper. Address it to the person who interviewed you. Be sure to spell the interviewer's name correctly. Call the company if you're not sure of the spelling. Then proofread your letter to make sure there aren't any mistakes.

A THANK-YOU LETTER

```
                              999 Bowers Street
                              Highland Lakes, NJ 07431
                              February 13, 199X

Mr. Charles Lindsay
Ace Sporting Goods Company
1515 Broad Street
Highland Lakes, NJ 07431

Dear Mr. Lindsay:

Thank you for the time and consideration shown
to me during my interview for the Assistant
Manager's job on Friday, February 11.

I feel confident that I could handle the
responsibilities of the job and would like you to
consider me as a serious applicant.

I look forward to hearing from you in the near
future.

                              Yours truly,

                              Randy Smith
                              Randy Smith
```

When you write a thank-you letter, state which job you're interested in and thank the interviewer for his or her time.

If you were given an employment test or an application form to take home, complete it and return it with your thank-you letter. Also send along any other documents the interviewer may have requested, such as a copy of your high school diploma.

If you haven't heard from the interviewer after two weeks, call and find out if the job has been filled. Wait longer if the interviewer told you it would take more time.

When you call, you may be told that the job has been filled or that no decision has been made. Even so, your call won't hurt your chances of getting the job. In fact, you may even improve your odds of getting it. It will show the employer that you're still interested. It will also keep your name in the interviewer's mind for this job or one that might open up in the future.

What Would You Do?

If you were Will Hoffman, how would you follow up on the interview for the mechanic's job? Write your response on the lines below.

_____
_____
_____
_____
_____

Then use the information in the story about Will to write a thank-you letter to Mr. Arnold. Use a separate sheet of paper for your letter. The company's address is Brownsville Motors, 123 Highway #7, Brownsville, IL 61734.

POINTS TO REMEMBER

In this section, you learned many tips that you can follow to have a winning interview. They include:

- making a good impression by taking special care with your appearance and behavior
- preparing to answer difficult questions
- knowing your legal rights as an applicant
- knowing when and how to end an interview
- following up after the interview

■ TAKING ✓ STOCK ■

WORKING VOCABULARY

Use the clues to fill in the crossword puzzle with the correct word or words from the list below.

civil rights
constitutional rights
discriminate
EEOC
hygiene
manual labor
profanity

ACROSS:
3. These are granted to you by the U.S. Constitution
5. Cleanliness that should be a part of grooming
7. To treat unfairly

DOWN:
1. These laws protect your constitutional rights
2. Work for which you use your hands
4. The federal agency that enforces civil rights laws
6. Bad language

56   Section Five

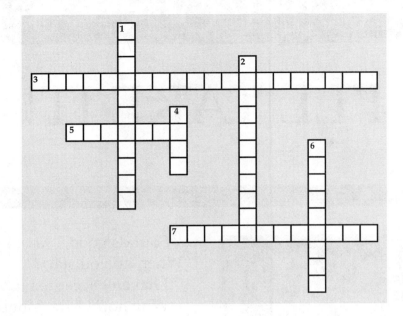

SKILLS FOR WORK

Your younger brother has a job interview. He has asked you for some interviewing tips. On the lines below, list five tips you would give him.

1. _____
2. _____
3. _____
4. _____
5. _____

YOU DECIDE

Suppose you were interviewed for a job yesterday. At the end of the interview, the interviewer told you that you didn't get the job because you lacked some of the qualifications. Would you still follow up? If so, what would you do? If not, explain your answer.

_____
_____

FINDING OUT MORE

Find a book or magazine on careers that includes information on interviewing. Read that information to add five extra tips to your list of how to dress and act on interviews.

1. _____
2. _____
3. _____
4. _____
5. _____

What was the source of this information?_____

_____

Did you find it helpful?_____

Why or why not? _____

_____

A Winning Interview   57

SECTION SIX

I'LL TAKE IT!

Mrs. Johnson and her daughter sipped tea in the kitchen. "I knew you'd find a job," Mrs. Johnson said. "Tell me about it."

"It's at the Corner Cafe in Clarksville," Linda said. "I'd work from 10 to 4. If I do a good job, I'll get a raise after a few months."

"Sounds good," Mrs. Johnson said. "When do you start?"

"I haven't accepted it," Linda said.

"Why not?" Mrs. Johnson asked.

"I need your advice before I make a decision," Linda said. "I'm not sure this job is the best one for me."

"Start by telling me what you like about it," Mrs. Johnson said.

"It seems like a good place to work. Everybody works well together. And I hear that the tips at lunch are big."

"Are there benefits?" Mrs. Johnson asked.

"Yes, I'd get a paid vacation," Linda replied. "And there's a good medical plan for me and the kids."

"It sounds like a good job to me," Mrs. Johnson said. "So why don't you want to take it?"

"I prefer to work closer to home," Linda said. "Being close to home and the kids is important to me. What would I do if they got sick?"

"You'd call me and I'd take care of them," Mrs. Johnson said.

"You're sure you wouldn't mind?"

"Of course not," Mrs. Johnson said. "I don't see them enough anyway."

"You're a life saver, Mom." ■

Linda had to think carefully before she accepted the job at the Corner Cafe. You have to give careful thought to the decision you make, too. When you must decide if a job is right for you, you should consider:

- what hours you would work
- where the job is located
- how much money you would take home
- what benefits the company provides
- how much money you would spend on job-related expenses
- the chance for advancement

THE RIGHT JOB FOR YOU

Linda's mother helped her weigh the pros and cons of taking the job at the Corner Cafe. Although the job seemed to be a good one, Linda was unsure about it because she wanted to work close to home. Her mother helped her see that the only reason she would rather have a job nearby was because of her children. By offering to provide child care when necessary, Mrs. Johnson solved Linda's problem.

When you are offered a job, how do you know if it is right for you? To decide, you should know what your needs are. Ask yourself the following questions. They will help you rate jobs and determine what's right for you.

- **What hours will I have to work?** Will I work regular hours? Will I work nights, weekends, or overtime?
- **Where is the job located?** How will I get to and from work? How much will transportation cost?
- **How much does the job pay?** What is the hourly or weekly wage?
- **What benefits come with the job?** Will the company provide medical insurance, paid vacations, and other benefits?
- **How much money will the job cost me?** What will I have to spend on transportation, food, clothing, and other costs?
- **What future does the job offer?** Are there chances for learning, training, or advancement?

It's unlikely that you will find a job that meets all of your wants and needs. But you can aim for a job that will meet your most important ones. For example, you may not find a high-paying job that offers training and a company child care center close to where you live. But if you're willing to travel a few miles, you may find a job that pays you enough to cover child care costs and offers training.

Giving up one benefit in favor of another is making a **trade-off.** In making a job decision you can live with, you give up the things that are least important to you.

Linda decided to go back to work when her children started school. In taking a job as a waitress, Linda felt that working close to home, having good benefits, and getting good pay were most important. The job she was offered met two of her three goals—good benefits and pay. She decided to take the job even though it

It is unlikely that you will find a job that meets all your needs. You will probably have to make trade-offs.

wasn't close to home. That's because Linda's other needs were more important to her. She felt that she needed the medical insurance and good pay to take care of her family.

In this section, you will take a closer look at each of the questions on page 59. By doing so, you will find out what things about a job mean the most to you. And you will learn which of these you're willing to trade off.

Making Choices

Here are five factors that go into making a job choice. On the numbered lines, list the factors in order of their importance to you. Number 1 should be the most important to you, and number 5 should be the least important.

Hours   Benefits
Location   Chance for
Salary   advancement

1. _____
2. _____
3. _____
4. _____
5. _____

WORKING HOURS

An important choice that many people have to make is the hours they work. Some people want to work during the day because they need to plan their schedules with spouses, child care or school, or available transportation. Some people choose specific hours so they can pursue outside interests or activities, such as attending school.

For example, Joe wanted to work nights so he could stay home during the day to care for his three young children. He needed to do that because his wife works half-days, and they can't afford to pay a babysitter. As a result, Joe got a job driving a bus at night.

Some companies provide flexible working hours for employees who need different schedules. Companies that offer **flextime** (FLEKS•tym), for example, allow employees to choose their own working hours (within certain limits) as long as they work a specific number of hours each week.

Other companies offer **shift work.** Shift work is found in industries that operate 24 hours a day. Employees usually work eight-hour shifts. These shifts may be early in the day, late at night, or at times in between.

Shift work is most common in manufacturing, transportation, and some service jobs, such as in hotels, airlines, and hospitals. This working arrangement is helpful to people who need time to do other things. For example, Jill goes to school in the morning. Her evening job as a clerk at a hospital gives her the time for her schoolwork.

Some people work flexible hours by taking part in **job sharing.** Job sharing requires that two people share the same job. Each person works on a part-time basis. Together, they hold down one full-time job.

When you consider a job, think about whether you are willing to work overtime. Some companies expect employees to work overtime. Before you accept a job, find out if you have to work overtime and how much you will be paid when you do.

A JOB'S LOCATION

Linda didn't mind working far from home as long as someone could take care of her children when they were sick or had a day off. If her mother hadn't offered to help, then Linda might have turned down the job because it was too far from home.

A job's location is important to most people. They don't want to work too far from home or at a place that's too difficult to get to. And they don't want to spend too much money traveling. For instance, many people who live in the country or in outlying areas do not want to spend time and money traveling long distances to a job in a town or city.

The amount of time you spend traveling to work, or **commuting** (kuh•MYOOT•ing), often depends on the type of transportation you use. Your time can vary depending on whether you drive; take a train, bus, or subway; ride a bike; or walk. However, the location of the job usually determines which type of transportation you can use to get there. For example, the Corner Cafe was not located along a public transportation route, so Linda realized that she would have to drive to and from work.

When you start looking for a job, ask yourself what kinds of dependable

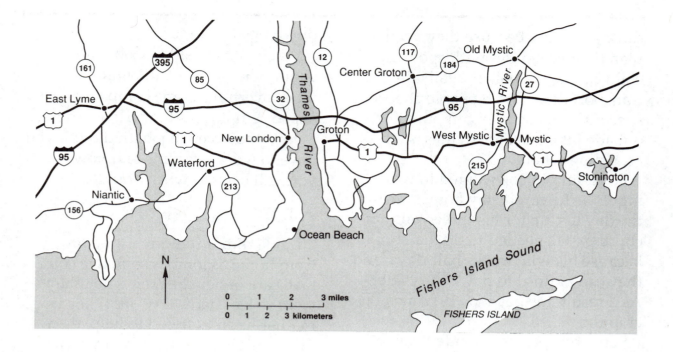

transportation are available to you. If you don't have a car, is there a bus or train stop near your home? Does the public transportation route near you take you directly to an area where you could get a job? Are there any jobs close enough that you could walk or ride a bike there?

If you're not sure what public transportation is available in your area, find out. Get schedules and route maps for the trains, buses, or subways near your home. You can get them from your local or county transportation department. See which ones stop near your home. And find out what areas they travel to and how long it takes to get there.

When you apply for a job, think about how you could get there. Is the job in an area that is convenient to get to? Or would it take you longer to get there than would be worthwhile for you?

You also need to think about the cost of traveling to and from a job. If you plan to take public transportation, find out how much the train, bus, or subway fare would cost you each day. Remember that weekly or monthly passes can save you money if you use public transportation to get to work every day.

If the job isn't near public transportation, then figure out how much it would cost you to drive. Be sure to include gas, parking, tolls, repairs, and insurance in your total driving costs.

Figuring out the cost of transportation is important. If getting to work costs you too much, the job may not be worth taking.

Reading a Map

You have two job interviews tomorrow. The first one is in the town of New London. The second one is in the town of Old Mystic. You live in the town of East Lyme. Use the map on page 62 to answer the following questions about driving to and from your interviews.

1. What roads would you take to get to the first interview?

   _____

   _____

2. Judging by the scale on the map, how many miles away is your town from the first interview?

   _____

   _____

3. If you went home after the first interview, what roads would you take to get to the second interview from your home?

   _____

   _____

4. How many miles away is your town from the second interview?

   _____

   _____

5. Which job would be easier to get to? Explain why.

   _____

   _____

WHAT DOES IT PAY?

What a job pays, the **salary** or wages, is one of the most important things to consider about any job. When you are given a salary figure, make sure that this figure is your **gross pay.** Gross pay is the pay you earn before **deductions** (dih•DUK•shuns) are taken out. Your **net pay** or **take-home pay** is the amount of money you would actually take home.

The biggest deductions from your gross pay are for federal and state **income taxes.** These are taxes that you must pay on your earnings. In general, the more money you make, the higher your federal and state taxes. However, you pay a lower tax if you have children or other family members to support.

Other deductions from gross pay may include local taxes, Social Security, unemployment insurance, union dues, and retirement payments. These deductions and income taxes add up. In fact, most people must pay between 20 and 25 percent of their salary for deductions. If an employer tells you what your gross pay will be, multiply the figure by 20 to 25 percent. Then subtract the number you get from your gross pay. That will give you a good idea of how much pay you will take home.

PAYMENT METHODS

Employers pay their workers differently. The most common ways include:

- **Hourly pay.** You are paid a set amount for each hour you work. You may have to punch a **time clock** when you begin and end work each day.
- **A straight salary.** With a salary, the amount of money you make may be stated as a weekly, monthly, or yearly figure.
- **Tips.** Some service workers, such as waiters and waitresses,

hairdressers, and taxi drivers, receive **tips** from their customers. Because of the tips, these workers often get lower hourly pay than employees in other jobs.
- **Commission.** In many sales jobs, employees are paid a salary plus a **commission** (kuh•MIHSH•un). This is a percentage of the amount of money the salesperson earns for the company. Some salesworkers receive no salary. They are paid only a commission.

In some jobs, most or all of your pay may be in the form of tips or a commission. If that's the case, keep in mind that the amount you earn may vary greatly from one week to another. Some workers like to earn commissions or receive tips. That's because the more customers they serve, the more money they make.

How Much Would You Make?

You have seen three ads for jobs that interest you. Before you answer them, you want to figure out how much your gross pay and your take-home pay would be for each job.

Figure out the pay for the three jobs below. Use 20 percent as the amount of your deductions before take-home pay.

Job #1: It pays $7.50 an hour for a 40-hour work week.

The weekly gross pay would be _____.

The weekly take-home pay would be _____.

Job #2: It pays $18,200 per year (there are 52 weeks in a year).

The weekly gross pay would be _____.

The weekly take-home pay would be _____.

Job #3: It pays $8.50 an hour for a 35-hour work week.

The weekly gross pay would be _____.

The weekly take-home pay would be _____.

JOB BENEFITS

Most full-time workers are paid more than money for their work. They also receive **fringe benefits.** Fringe benefits are forms of payment that decrease workers' out-of-pocket expenses. They also improve workers' morale. For example, many companies provide medical insurance for their employees. This helps employees pay their medical bills.

When a company provides you with benefits, you may save hundreds of dollars a year in expenses. That's why it's important to consider the value of fringe benefits when you compare jobs.

People's choices regarding fringe benefits differ greatly. To Linda, medical insurance was important. Another person may be more concerned about paid vacations or sick time.

When you consider a job, find out

about the fringe benefits. Ask yourself if the company provides the benefits that are most important to you.

TYPES OF BENEFITS

Companies may offer many different kinds of fringe benefits. The most common ones include:

- **Paid vacation.** The company pays you for a certain number of days each year that you are on vacation. Workers are usually allowed to take a vacation of one to two weeks one year after they're hired.
- **Paid sick time.** The company pays you for a certain number of days each year that you are out sick.
- **Paid personal time.** The company pays you for a certain number of days each year when you're out taking care of personal business.
- **Medical/dental insurance.** The company contributes to a health insurance plan that covers hospital, doctor, and dentist bills for you and your family.
- **Life insurance.** The company provides a group **insurance policy** for its employees. If you die while employed by the company, the insurance money is paid to the person you have chosen, or your **beneficiary** (ben•uh•FIHSH•ee•er•ee).
- **Disability insurance.** The company pays for insurance for you in case you become ill or disabled and can't work.
- **Maternity/paternity leave.** The company pays your salary for a certain time period while you are home with your newborn child.
- **Pension plan.** The company sets aside money for you that you can collect when you retire.
- **Child care.** The company pays for all or part of the child care costs for its workers who have children. Some companies provide on-site child care, which may be free or inexpensive for all workers.

Rating Fringe Benefits

On the lines below, list the five fringe benefits that matter most to you. Use benefits from the list on this page. Put them in order of importance. Number 1 should be the most important to you, and number 5 should be the least important.

1. _____
2. _____
3. _____
4. _____
5. _____

JOB COSTS

When people figure out what they will earn at certain jobs, many of them don't consider their job-related expenses. No matter what job you take, you will have to spend some money on work-related expenses.

You already know that transportation can be a big expense

I'll Take It! 65

when you work. You may also have to buy special clothing, tools, or equipment. Some jobs, such as nurse, security officer, and food worker, require special uniforms. If you work in an office, your clothing may have to meet certain dress codes. Some salespeople must have and keep up their own cars. All of these expenses can reduce the amount of money you have left to spend.

Food is also a job-related expense. According to law, full-time workers must have a mealtime break if they work more than four hours a day. You need to consider where you will eat that meal and about how much your food will cost you each week. For example, does the company have a lunchroom where you can eat a lunch you bring from home? Or would you have to buy your lunch each day? How much would that cost?

Workers who are parents may have to spend money for babysitters or child care while they work. If you have children who will need to be cared for while you work, you must figure out how much it will cost. Some large companies offer child-care services for their employees' children.

You may have to consider other job-related expenses. If you work in a state or city other than the one you live in, you might have to pay a nonresident income tax. This out-of-state tax may not be taken out of your pay, so you may have to set aside money to pay this income tax each year. Similarly, if your union dues or pension plan payments aren't subtracted from your gross pay, you may have to pay those fees out of your take-home pay.

A JOB'S FUTURE

If you like a certain job, then you should consider what kind of future the job might offer. At some point, you will want a better job with better pay. Companies recognize that people have this need, so many companies have a policy of promoting their valuable workers.

When you apply for a job, try to find out what you can look forward to with the company. You might ask if the company has an annual raise policy or a merit raise policy in which good workers receive raises. In addition, you might ask whether you could get further training or learn new skills. The more skills you have, the more valuable you will be to your employer. And the more valuable you are, the better your chances for raises and **promotions,** which are advances in position within a company.

When you are interviewed, don't be afraid to ask direct questions. For example, you might ask how often people advance in their jobs with the company. Another question is whether good workers get raises and promotions. By asking these questions, you will show the employer that you care about your future and that you're interested in a future with the company.

POINTS TO REMEMBER

In this section, you learned that there are many things to think about when you look for a job. Some of the most important include:

- deciding what hours you need to work
- considering how you would get to work and how much it would cost
- finding out about the pay and benefits of the job
- figuring out how much money you would spend on work-related items
- evaluating the chances for future advancement

TAKING ✓ STOCK

WORKING VOCABULARY

Fill in the blanks beside each definition with the correct word or words from the list below. When you complete the blanks, the circled letters will spell a very important job consideration. Note: There are more words than definitions.

beneficiary   **job sharing**
commission   **net pay**
commute   **promotion**
deduction   **salary**
flextime   **shift work**
fringe benefit   **take-home pay**
gross pay   **time clock**
income tax   **tip**
insurance policy   **trade-off**

1. _ _ _ (_) _ _ _ _ _ _

   An arrangement in which two people work part-time in the same job

2. _ _ _ (_) _ _ - _ _ _

   To give up something in order to have another

3. _ (_) _ _ _ _ _ _

   When people work hours that are earlier or later than usual

4. _ (_) _ _ - _ _ _ _ _ _ _

   The pay you get after deductions

5. _ _ _ _ _ _ _ _ _ (_) _

   The person you have chosen to receive the insurance money from your life insurance policy

6. _ _ _ _ _ _ _ (_) _

   The money you earn before deductions are taken out

7. What job consideration do the circled letters spell?

   _ _ _ _ _ _

SKILLS FOR WORK

You have been offered a job. List five factors you would consider carefully when you make your decision.

1. _____
2. _____
3. _____
4. _____
5. _____

I'll Take It!   67

YOU DECIDE

When you look for a job, you will have to make many choices. Imagine you could choose from a list of benefits. The choices are listed below. Pick one benefit from each pair and explain why you chose it.

Disability Insurance   or   Pension Plan

_____
_____
_____

Parental Leave   or   Paid Personal Time

_____
_____
_____

Flexible Hours   or   Overtime Pay

_____
_____
_____

Medical Insurance   or   Life Insurance

_____
_____
_____

FINDING OUT MORE

Talk to three friends or relatives who work. Ask them to give each of the following factors in choosing a job a rating from 1 to 5. Number 1 should be the most important. Number 5 should be the least important.

Location
Hours
Salary
Benefits
Chance for advancement

	Person #1	Person #2	Person #3
1.	_____	_____	_____
2.	_____	_____	_____
3.	_____	_____	_____
4.	_____	_____	_____
5.	_____	_____	_____

1. Which preference was most popular?
   _____

2. Which was least popular?
   _____

3. Compare these ratings to yours on page 60. What did you list as your number 1 choice?
   _____

4. What did you list as your number 5 choice?
   _____

5. Why do you think people are so different (or so alike, depending on the results of your survey)?
   _____
   _____
   _____

SECTION SEVEN

THE WORLD OF WORK

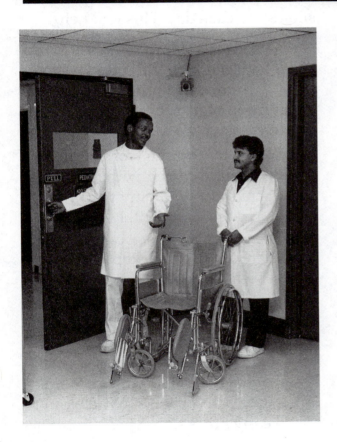

When Alex was leaving the hospital ward, he met Luis. Alex had just finished his first morning working as an orderly. Luis had been an orderly for more than two years.

"Hi, my name is Luis," Luis said. "You must be Alex."

"That's right," Alex said.

"So, did everything go alright your first morning?" Luis asked.

"I was so uptight this morning that I thought I would do everything wrong," Alex said. "But it went OK."

"This is a pretty good place to work," Luis said. "The people are really nice."

"Yeah, everybody's helpful," Alex said. "Mr. Ortiz is a great manager. He showed me where everything was and how to do each job."

"Ortiz is great," Luis said. "If you ever have a problem or a question, you can talk to him. And he always lets you know how you're doing."

"He already did," Alex said. "He told me I was doing a good job."

"Then I guess you're not too nervous any more," Luis said, with a smile.

"No," Alex laughed. "I'm feeling a lot better than I did this morning."

"Are you on your way to lunch?" Luis asked.

Alex nodded.

"Why don't you eat with me and some of the other guys?" Luis said. "I'll show you where things are and introduce you around."

"That sounds good," Alex said, as he followed Luis to the cafeteria. ∎

Alex had quite a few adjustments to make when he started his new job. When you start a new job, you should:

- learn the details of your job and the company
- learn about company rules and policies
- fill out a Form W-4
- learn how to use a time card or a timesheet
- find out when to expect your first paycheck

DAY ONE

When you start a new job, you may find that your first day is like Alex's. He liked his job and he felt comfortable there. That doesn't mean he won't have an **adjustment period.** When starting a new job, an employee must get used to a new routine and new people.

If you don't like your new job the first day, or even the first month, it doesn't mean that you never will. Adjusting to change can be difficult. That's why you should try to stick with it for at least a few months.

Your day will probably begin with a discussion between you and your boss. Your boss will explain the tasks you're responsible for. And you will ask questions so that you understand how to do things.

At the hospital, Alex's boss gave him a written **job description** that listed all of his duties. They went over the description together and Mr. Ortiz answered Alex's questions. If you are given a job description, it's a good idea to go over it in detail with your boss.

Some large companies give new employees an **orientation** (or•ee•un•TAY•shun) **day.** During that day, employees learn about the job and the company. This often takes place before an employee's first working day.

No matter how you spend your first day, try to find out what you should do each day. This will help you avoid making mistakes in the future. Ask questions, such as:

- Who will evaluate my work? Who will train me?
- Will anyone besides my supervisor give me work? Will anyone be working with me?
- Where should I do my work?
- What equipment will I have to use?
- Where are supplies kept? How do I get what I need?
- What hours should I work? What time should I check in and out? Should I punch a time clock?
- When should I take lunch and breaks? How much time do I have for lunch and breaks? Where can I take my breaks?

Most new employees spend some time the first day meeting co-workers. Alex's meeting with Luis happened by chance. In many offices, a boss or co-worker shows a new employee around and introduces him or her to the other people who work there.

If you tour the workplace, look at where people are and what they're doing. Notice how people keep their

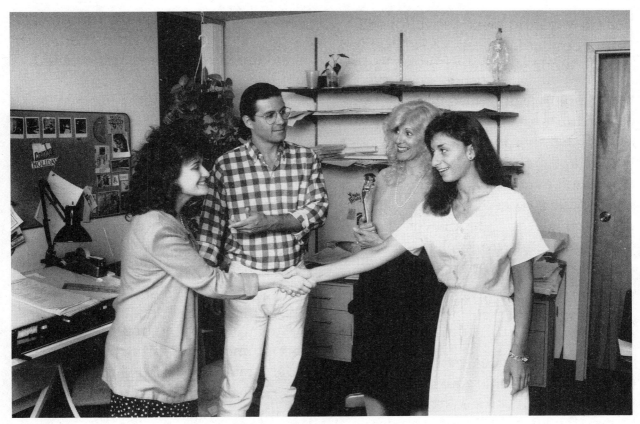

When you start a new job, be prepared to meet your co-workers. Don't expect to remember all of their names right away.

work spaces and what they're wearing. Observing what others do can help you fit in more easily.

The hospital where Alex and Luis work requires its employees to wear uniforms. Some companies have different dress codes. For example, some employers require all men to wear shirts with collars. Others may not allow employees to wear jeans or sneakers.

Companies may also have other policies that their workers must know and follow. Some of the most common ones concern working hours, vacation, personal days, and sick leave. Find out if these policies are written down anywhere.

COMPANY POLICIES

Some companies have **employee manuals** that explain the company rules. These written guides may also include information about fringe benefits, the structure of the company, and ways to apply for new positions within the company.

If your company has an employee manual, look through it when you start work. That way you will learn the basic policies and rules. You don't have to memorize the manual. But keep it nearby in case you need it.

Instead of a manual, smaller companies may provide their employees with folders containing

The World of Work

lists of rules. Other employers may not have much in writing. If that's the case, then you will have to ask questions to find out information.

When you ask questions, observe the company chain of command. In other words, don't approach your boss's boss about an issue until you've approached your boss first. And don't ever *assume* anything. It's much better to keep asking questions until you get the right answer, than to guess and get it wrong.

UNDERSTANDING A FORM W-4

In Section 6 you learned that the federal government requires all people to pay income taxes on the money they earn. The government uses the money from these taxes to pay for its services.

On every new job you start, you will have to fill out a **withholding form.** This form allows your employer to take out money from your salary for federal and other income taxes. A withholding form is also called a **Form W-4.**

To fill out the Form W-4 correctly, you have to know how many **allowances** to declare. You can claim an allowance for each person, including yourself, whom you support. For each allowance you claim, you will have less tax deducted from your pay. If you are a single parent who pays most of the household expenses, you may be able to claim an allowance as **head of household.**

The Form W-4 comes with an attached worksheet, as shown on pages 73 and 74. In this example, Alex has claimed allowances for himself and his wife.

The second page of the Form W-4 includes a special worksheet (see page 74). People may need to use the worksheet if they **itemize** (EYE•tuh•myz), or list one by one, income tax deductions. People may also need to use the worksheet if their earnings are above a certain level. These worksheets help you make sure you're having the right amount of money deducted.

An employee who doesn't earn enough money in one year to owe any federal tax may claim **exempt** (ihg•ZEMPT) status. You can find out if you meet the requirements to be in this category by contacting your local Internal Revenue Service office.

Practice Filling Out a Form W-4

Imagine that you have just started a new job. Your new employer has handed you a copy of a Form W-4 to fill out.

Complete the form on page 75. Fill it out as you would if you didn't itemize deductions and have exempt status.

USING TIME CARDS AND TIMESHEETS

If you work a full day, you should be paid for a full day. By filling in a **time card** or a **timesheet** each day,

199X Form W-4

Department of the Treasury
Internal Revenue Service

Purpose. Complete Form W-4 so that your employer can withhold the correct amount of Federal income tax from your pay.

Exemption From Withholding. Read line 6 of the certificate below to see if you can claim exempt status. *If exempt, complete line 6; but do not complete lines 4 and 5.* No Federal income tax will be withheld from your pay. This exemption expires February 15, 199X.

Basic Instructions. Employees who are not exempt should complete the Personal Allowances Worksheet. Additional worksheets are provided on page 2 for employees to adjust their withholding allowances based on itemized deductions, adjustments to income, or two-earner/two-job situations. Complete all worksheets that apply to your situation. The worksheets will help you figure the number of withholding allowances you are entitled to claim. However, you may claim fewer allowances than this.

Head of Household. Generally, you may claim head of household filing status on your tax return only if you are unmarried and pay more than 50% of the costs of keeping up a home for yourself and your dependent(s) or other qualifying individuals.

Nonwage Income. If you have a large amount of nonwage income, such as interest or dividends, you should consider making estimated tax payments using Form 1040-ES. Otherwise, you may find that you owe additional tax at the end of the year.

Two-Earner/Two-Jobs. If you have a working spouse or more than one job, figure the total number of allowances you are entitled to claim on all jobs using worksheets from only one Form W-4. This total should be divided among all jobs. Your withholding will usually be most accurate when all allowances are claimed on the W-4 filed for the highest paying job and zero allowances are claimed for the others.

Advance Earned Income Credit. If you are eligible for this credit, you can receive it added to your paycheck throughout the year. For details, obtain Form W-5 from your employer.

Check Your Withholding. After your W-4 takes effect, you can use **Publication 919,** Is My Withholding Correct for 199X?, to see how the dollar amount you are having withheld compares to your estimated total annual tax. Call 1-800-424-3676 (in Hawaii and Alaska, check your local telephone directory) to order this publication. Check your local telephone directory for the IRS assistance number if you need further help.

Personal Allowances Worksheet

A	Enter "1" for **yourself** if no one else can claim you as a dependent . . . . **A**	*1*
B	Enter "1" if: { 1. You are single and have only one job; or 2. You are married, have only one job, and your spouse does not work; or 3. Your wages from a second job or your spouse's wages (or the total of both) are $2,500 or less. } . . . . . . **B**	*1*
C	Enter "1" for your **spouse.** But, you may choose to enter "0" if you are married and have either a working spouse or more than one job (this may help you avoid having too little tax withheld) . . . . **C**	
D	Enter number of **dependents** (other than your spouse or yourself) whom you will claim on your tax return . . . . . **D**	
E	Enter "1" if you will file as a **head of household** on your tax return (see conditions under "Head of Household," above) . . **E**	
F	Enter "1" if you have at least $1,500 of **child or dependent care expenses** for which you plan to claim a credit . . . **F**	
G	Add lines A through F and enter total here . . . . ▶ **G**	*2*

For accuracy, do all worksheets that apply.
- If you plan to **itemize or claim adjustments to income** and want to reduce your withholding, turn to the Deductions and Adjustments Worksheet on page 2.
- If you are **single** and have **more than one job** and your combined earnings from all jobs exceed $25,000 OR if you are **married** and have a **working spouse or more than one job,** and the combined earnings from all jobs exceed $44,000, then turn to the Two-Earner/Two-Job Worksheet on page 2 if you want to avoid having too little tax withheld.
- If **neither** of the above situations applies to you, **stop here** and enter the number from line G on line 4 of Form W-4 below.

--------- Cut here and give the certificate to your employer. Keep the top portion for your records. ---------

Form **W-4** Department of the Treasury Internal Revenue Service	**Employee's Withholding Allowance Certificate** ▶ For Privacy Act and Paperwork Reduction Act Notice, see reverse.	OMB No. 1545-0010 **199X**

1 Type or print your first name and middle initial *Alex*	Last name *Davis*	**2** Your social security number *178-49-5237*
Home address (number and street or rural route) *229 Heather Drive*	**3** Marital status	☐ Single ☑ Married ☐ Married, but withhold at higher Single rate.
City or town, state, and ZIP code *Monroe, GA 30909*		*Note: If married, but legally separated, or spouse is a nonresident alien, check the Single box.*

4 Total number of allowances you are claiming (from line G above or from the Worksheets on back if they apply) . . . **4**
5 Additional amount, if any, you want deducted from each pay . . . . **5** $
6 I claim exemption from withholding and I certify that I meet **ALL** of the following conditions for exemption:
- Last year I had a right to a refund of **ALL** Federal income tax withheld because I had **NO** tax liability; **AND**
- This year I expect a refund of **ALL** Federal income tax withheld because I expect to have **NO** tax liability; **AND**
- This year if my income exceeds $500 and includes nonwage income, another person cannot claim me as a dependent.

If you meet all of the above conditions, enter the year effective and "EXEMPT" here . . . . ▶ **6** 19
7 Are you a full-time student? (**Note:** *Full-time students are not automatically exempt.*) . . . . **7** ☐ Yes ☐ No

Under penalties of perjury, I certify that I am entitled to the number of withholding allowances claimed on this certificate or entitled to claim exempt status.

Employee's signature ▶ *Alex Davis*   Date ▶ *March 29*, 19*9X*

8 Employer's name and address (**Employer:** Complete 8 and 10 **only if** sending to IRS) | **9** Office code (optional) | **10** Employer identification number

The World of Work

Form W-4 (199X) Page 2

Deductions and Adjustments Worksheet

Note: *Use this worksheet only if you plan to itemize deductions or claim adjustments to income on your 199X tax return.*

1. Enter an estimate of your 199X itemized deductions. These include: qualifying home mortgage interest, 10% of personal interest, charitable contributions, state and local taxes (but not sales taxes), medical expenses in excess of 7.5% of your income, and miscellaneous deductions (most miscellaneous deductions are now deductible only in excess of 2% of your income) . . . . **1** $ _____

2. Enter: $5,450 if married filing jointly or qualifying widow(er)
           $4,750 if head of household
           $3,250 if single
           $2,725 if married filing separately . . . . **2** $ _____

3. **Subtract** line 2 from line 1. If line 2 is greater than line 1, enter zero . . . . . **3** $ _____
4. Enter an estimate of your 199X adjustments to income. These include alimony paid and deductible IRA contributions . . **4** $ _____
5. **Add** lines 3 and 4 and enter the total . . . . **5** $ _____
6. Enter an estimate of your 199X nonwage income (such as dividends or interest income) . . **6** $ _____
7. **Subtract** line 6 from line 5. Enter the result, but not less than zero . . . . . **7** $ _____
8. **Divide** the amount on line 7 by $2,000 and enter the result here. Drop any fraction . . **8** _____
9. Enter the number from Personal Allowances Worksheet, line G, on page 1 . . . . . **9** _____
10. **Add** lines 8 and 9 and enter the total here. If you plan to use the Two-Earner/Two-Job Worksheet, also enter the total on line 1, below. Otherwise, **stop here** and enter this total on Form W-4, line 4 on page 1 . . . **10** _____

Two-Earner/Two-Job Worksheet

Note: *Use this worksheet only if the instructions at line G on page 1 direct you here.*

1. Enter the number from line G on page 1 (or from line 10 above if you used the Deductions and Adjustments Worksheet) . **1** _____
2. Find the number in **Table 1** below that applies to the **LOWEST** paying job and enter it here . . . . . **2** _____
3. If line 1 is **GREATER THAN OR EQUAL TO** line 2, subtract line 2 from line 1. Enter the result here (if zero, enter "0") and on Form W-4, line 4, on page 1. **DO NOT** use the rest of this worksheet . . . . . **3** _____

Note: *If line 1 is LESS THAN line 2, enter "0" on Form W-4, line 4, on page 1. Complete lines 4–9 to calculate the additional dollar withholding necessary to avoid a year-end tax bill.*

4. Enter the number from line 2 of this worksheet . . . . **4** _____
5. Enter the number from line 1 of this worksheet . . . . **5** _____
6. **Subtract** line 5 from line 4 . . . . **6** _____
7. Find the amount in **Table 2** below that applies to the **HIGHEST** paying job and enter it here . . . . **7** $ _____
8. **Multiply** line 7 by line 6 and enter the result here. This is the additional annual withholding amount needed . . **8** $ _____
9. Divide line 8 by the number of pay periods each year. (For example, divide by 26 if you are paid every other week.) Enter the result here and on Form W-4, line 5, page 1. This is the additional amount to be withheld from each paycheck . . **9** $ _____

Table 1: Two-Earner/Two-Job Worksheet

Married Filing Jointly		All Others	
If wages from **LOWEST** paying job are—	Enter on line 2 above	If wages from **LOWEST** paying job are—	Enter on line 2 above
0 - $4,000	0	0 - $4,000	0
4,001 - 8,000	1	4,001 - 8,000	1
8,001 - 19,000	2	8,001 - 14,000	2
19,001 - 23,000	3	14,001 - 16,000	3
23,001 - 25,000	4	16,001 - 21,000	4
25,001 - 27,000	5	21,001 and over	5
27,001 - 29,000	6		
29,001 - 35,000	7		
35,001 - 41,000	8		
41,001 - 46,000	9		
46,001 and over	10		

Table 2: Two-Earner/Two-Job Worksheet

Married Filing Jointly		All Others	
If wages from **HIGHEST** paying job are—	Enter on line 7 above	If wages from **HIGHEST** paying job are—	Enter on line 7 above
0 - $44,000	$310	0 - $25,000	$310
44,001 - 90,000	570	25,001 - 52,000	570
90,001 and over	680	52,001 and over	680

Privacy Act and Paperwork Reduction Act Notice.—We ask for this information to carry out the Internal Revenue laws of the United States. We may give the information to the Department of Justice for civil or criminal litigation and to cities, states, and the District of Columbia for use in administering their tax laws. You are required to give this information to your employer.

The time needed to complete this form will vary depending on individual circumstances. The estimated average time is: **Recordkeeping** 46 min., **Learning about the law or the form** 10 min., **Preparing the form** 70 min. If you have comments concerning the accuracy of these time estimates or suggestions for making this form more simple, we would be happy to hear from you. You can write to the **Internal Revenue Service,** Washington, DC 20224, Attn: IRS Reports Clearance Officer, T:FP; or the **Office of Management and Budget,** Paperwork Reduction Project (1545-0010), Washington, DC 20503.

☆ U.S. Government Printing Office:1989-245-066

 **Form W-4**

Purpose. Complete Form W-4 so that your employer can withhold the correct amount of Federal income tax from your pay.

Exemption From Withholding. Read line 6 of the certificate below to see if you can claim exempt status. *If exempt, complete line 6; but do not complete lines 4 and 5.* No Federal income tax will be withheld from your pay. This exemption expires February 15, 199X.

Basic Instructions. Employees who are not exempt should complete the Personal Allowances Worksheet. Additional worksheets are provided on page 2 for employees to adjust their withholding allowances based on itemized deductions, adjustments to income, or two-earner/two-job situations. Complete all worksheets that apply to your situation. The worksheets will help you figure the number of withholding allowances you are entitled to claim. However, you may claim fewer allowances than this.

Head of Household. Generally, you may claim head of household filing status on your tax return only if you are unmarried and pay more than 50% of the costs of keeping up a home for yourself and your dependent(s) or other qualifying individuals.

Nonwage Income. If you have a large amount of nonwage income, such as interest or dividends, you should consider making estimated tax payments using Form 1040-ES. Otherwise, you may find that you owe additional tax at the end of the year.

Two-Earner/Two-Jobs. If you have a working spouse or more than one job, figure the total number of allowances you are entitled to claim on all jobs using worksheets from only one Form W-4. This total should be divided among all jobs. Your withholding will usually be most accurate when all allowances are claimed on the W-4 filed for the highest paying job and zero allowances are claimed for the others.

Advance Earned Income Credit. If you are eligible for this credit, you can receive it added to your paycheck throughout the year. For details, obtain Form W-5 from your employer.

Check Your Withholding. After your W-4 takes effect, you can use **Publication 919,** Is My Withholding Correct for 199X?, to see how the dollar amount you are having withheld compares to your estimated total annual tax. Call 1-800-424-3676 (in Hawaii and Alaska, check your local telephone directory) to order this publication. Check your local telephone directory for the IRS assistance number if you need further help.

Personal Allowances Worksheet

A	Enter "1" for **yourself** if no one else can claim you as a dependent	A _____
B	Enter "1" if: { 1. You are single and have only one job; or 2. You are married, have only one job, and your spouse does not work; or 3. Your wages from a second job or your spouse's wages (or the total of both) are $2,500 or less. }	B _____
C	Enter "1" for your **spouse.** But, you may choose to enter "0" if you are married and have either a working spouse or more than one job (this may help you avoid having too little tax withheld)	C _____
D	Enter number of **dependents** (other than your spouse or yourself) whom you will claim on your tax return	D _____
E	Enter "1" if you will file as a **head of household** on your tax return (see conditions under "Head of Household," above) . .	E _____
F	Enter "1" if you have at least $1,500 of **child or dependent care expenses** for which you plan to claim a credit	F _____
G	Add lines A through F and enter total here . . . . ▶	G _____

For accuracy, do all worksheets that apply.
- If you plan to **itemize or claim adjustments to income** and want to reduce your withholding, turn to the Deductions and Adjustments Worksheet on page 2.
- If you are **single** and have **more than one job** and your combined earnings from all jobs exceed $25,000 OR if you are **married** and have a **working spouse or more than one job,** and the combined earnings from all jobs exceed $44,000, then turn to the Two-Earner/Two-Job Worksheet on page 2 if you want to avoid having too little tax withheld.
- If **neither** of the above situations applies to you, **stop here** and enter the number from line G on line 4 of Form W-4 below.

----- Cut here and give the certificate to your employer. Keep the top portion for your records. -----

Form W-4
Department of the Treasury
Internal Revenue Service

Employee's Withholding Allowance Certificate
▶ For Privacy Act and Paperwork Reduction Act Notice, see reverse.

OMB No. 1545-0010
199X

1 Type or print your first name and middle initial	Last name	2 Your social security number
Home address (number and street or rural route)	3 Marital status { ☐ Single ☐ Married ☐ Married, but withhold at higher Single rate. Note: *If married, but legally separated, or spouse is a nonresident alien, check the Single box.*	
City or town, state, and ZIP code		

4	Total number of allowances you are claiming (from line G above or from the Worksheets on back if they apply) . . .	4	
5	Additional amount, if any, you want deducted from each pay	5	$

6 I claim exemption from withholding and I certify that I meet **ALL** of the following conditions for exemption:
- Last year I had a right to a refund of **ALL** Federal income tax withheld because I had **NO** tax liability; **AND**
- This year I expect a refund of **ALL** Federal income tax withheld because I expect to have **NO** tax liability; **AND**
- This year if my income exceeds $500 and includes nonwage income, another person cannot claim me as a dependent.

If you meet all of the above conditions, enter the year effective and "EXEMPT" here . . . . . ▶ | 6 | 19

7 Are you a full-time student? (**Note:** *Full-time students are not automatically exempt.*) . . . . | 7 ☐ Yes ☐ No

Under penalties of perjury, I certify that I am entitled to the number of withholding allowances claimed on this certificate or entitled to claim exempt status.

Employee's signature ▶ _____ Date ▶ _____, 19 ____

8 Employer's name and address (**Employer:** Complete 8 and 10 **only if sending to IRS**)	9 Office code (optional)	10 Employer identification number

The World of Work 75

you can keep track of the hours and days you work. Then you and your employer will know how much you should be paid.

Time cards are used in factories and many other workplaces that pay by the hour. Every day that you work, you fill in the time card with the date, the time you started work (in the *In* column), and the time you stopped work (in the *Out* column).

At the end of the week or **pay period,** you figure out how many hours you worked each day (in the *Hours* column). Then you add up all the hours to get the total number of hours worked.

In some workplaces, time clocks are used to stamp the time of day when employees arrive and leave. Employees do this by inserting a time card into the machine at the beginning and the end of the workday.

In the hospital, employees don't use time cards. They use timesheets instead. Timesheets are often used in jobs where workers are paid a weekly salary. In his job, Alex works at least 35 hours a week. He gets an hour for lunch each day. His paycheck won't go up or down if he works an hour more or less each week.

Understanding a Time Card

The following time card shows you what hours Melanie Cooper worked the week ending July 20. Read the time card and answer the following questions. Use a calculator if you need to do so.

WEEKLY TIME CARD

Name: Melanie Cooper
Week Ending: July 20

DAY	IN	OUT	HOURS
Monday	8:00	4:00	8
Tuesday	7:45	4:15	8½
Wednesday	8:00	4:30	
Thursday	7:30	4:30	
Friday	8:00	4:00	

1. How many hours did Melanie work on Wednesday? _____
2. How many hours did she work on Thursday? _____
3. How many hours did she work on Friday? _____
4. How many hours total did Melanie work this week? _____

INSURANCE FORMS

Many workers feel that health insurance is the most valuable of all job benefits. Health care and insurance costs have risen greatly over the last 10 years.

About 9 out of 10 companies provide health insurance for their full-time employees. This saves workers money and contributes to their families' peace of mind. When you look for a job, it's important to compare the types and cost of insurance you're offered.

Companies, too, benefit from providing health insurance to employees. Chances are that workers will be happier on their jobs if they receive good benefits.

Alex was very concerned about medical insurance, because he needed it for both himself and his wife. He found out that for him health insurance is provided free of charge by his company. For a small fee, his wife would be covered, too.

In order to get health benefits, new workers usually must fill out insurance **enrollment forms.** Alex went to the personnel department to fill his out the first day. On the form, he filled in details about his health history as well as his wife's.

When you fill out an enrollment form, take your time and answer every question completely. If you make a mistake or leave out information, it could cause problems later on. These forms can be very complex. You might want to ask a personnel or benefits employee to help you with the form.

HOW TO COMPARE HEALTH INSURANCE

Many companies offer employees a choice between two types of health insurance. One is **traditional health care insurance** and the other is a **health maintenance organization** (HMO). Let's take a close look at each one.

Traditional Health Care Insurance

This protects people from major medical expenses and loss of income due to health-related problems. The company you work for could pay for the whole plan. Or it might require workers to pay part of the cost. This is called a **co-pay** plan. Generally you must be employed with a company for at least 30 days before you are eligible for coverage.

Whether you pay for part of the plan or not, your benefits don't begin until you pay a certain part of the cost of your own medical care. The amount you must pay is called the **deductible** (dih•DUK•tuh•bul). For example, if you have a $100 deductible plan, you would pay the first $100 of your medical bills. The insurance company would pay some or all of the rest.

In these plans, people may first have to pay their own bills. If they do, they file claim forms with the insurance company and get a certain amount of the money back.

Most basic plans include the following types of coverage:

- **Hospital and surgical insurance.** This pays for all or part of hospital bills and surgeons' fees as well as expenses from hospital stays.
- **Medical expense insurance.** This pays for doctors' fees for office visits and routine services.
- **Outpatient insurance.** This pays for treatment of illness or injury

without a hospital stay.
- **Major medical insurance.** This pays for some of the expenses that are not covered by other types of coverage.

Health Maintenance Organization

These organizations cover the same things as traditional health care insurance, but they operate in a different way. An HMO is a group or **association** (uh•so•see•AY•shun) of doctors who have organized to provide low-cost health care. The idea behind HMOs is that regular visits to the doctor prevent serious illnesses that can result in expensive hospital costs.

If you choose an HMO, when you need medical care you must first go to a doctor who is a member of your HMO group. You also must choose from a list of member hospitals, when possible. Then you can see any other doctor as long as you get a **referral** (rih•FUR•ul) from your main physician. And you can go to any hospital in an emergency.

Depending on the plan and your company's policy, you may have to pay part of the cost of the HMO. Although co-payment may be required in an HMO, there is no deductible. You pay nothing or a very small fee for medical services. You can also get services such as checkups without laying out any money because the service has already been paid for.

If your company offers both types of plans, pick the one that best meets your needs. For example, if you have a doctor you want to stay with, you may want to choose traditional health insurance. If you want to save more money on health care, you may want to choose an HMO.

 Choosing a Health Insurance Plan

You have just started a new job. The company offers its employees a traditional health insurance plan and an HMO plan. You have to decide today.

Which would you choose?

_____

_____

Explain why.

_____

_____

_____

_____

GETTING YOUR FIRST PAYCHECK

It's a good feeling to get your first paycheck. But some people are surprised when they see their take-home figure. This can happen if you expect to get your gross pay and forget about the deductions.

Look at the copy of Alex's paycheck on page 79. It includes the date, his name, and the name and address of the company and its bank.

Along with a paycheck comes a form called a **paystub.** It shows what deductions are taken from the gross pay.

Look at the copy of Alex's paystub.

As you can see, he earned $510 in gross pay. And he paid $123.07 for deductions. That includes his medical insurance, social security tax, federal income tax, disability/unemployment insurance, and state tax. His net, or take-home, pay is $386.93.

Compare the date on Alex's check with the date on the paystub next to the category "Pay Period Ending." As you can see, the paycheck is dated one full week after the end of the pay period. This means that *this* week's check is for *last* week's work.

Many companies pay on this schedule. It takes time for them to total each week's hours and write out the checks. For this reason, new employees may have to wait an extra week for their first paycheck. You should ask when you will be getting your first paycheck.

When you get your paycheck, you may have questions about the

MEMORIAL HOSPITAL
219 OAK STREET
RIVERSIDE, GA 30902

FIRST NATIONAL BANK
Downtown Office
Riverside, GA 30905

7972

DATE   Oct. 26, 199X
AMOUNT $386.93

PAY   Three Hundred Eighty-Six and 93/100 Dollars

TO THE ORDER OF   ALEX DAVIS
229 HEATHER DRIVE
MONROE, GA 30909

C. J. Evans

007971   000067894   12345678

Memorial Hospital   7972

PAY PERIOD ENDING: Oct. 19, 199X

EMPLOYEE NO: 4D-165   EMPLOYEE NAME: ALEX DAVIS   SOCIAL SEC. NUMBER: 178-49-5237

DESCRIPTION	CURRENT	YEAR-TO-DATE	DESCRIPTION	CURRENT	YEAR-TO-DATE
REGULAR	510.00	21,420.00	FICA	39.02	1,638.84
OVERTIME	.00	.00	FED. TAX	56.10	2,356.20
			DIS./UN.	7.65	321.30
			STATE TAX	15.30	642.60
			MED. INS.	5.00	210.00
TOTALS	510.00	21,420.00		Net Pay: 386.93 123.07	5,168.94

The World of Work

deductions. If you do, ask someone in the payroll or personnel department. The amounts taken out for taxes are based mainly on the information you provided on the Form W-4.

Look over your paystub every payday. Keep a record of the amounts that should be deducted. If these figures change, contact the payroll department to find out why.

UNDERSTANDING A FORM W-2

Each January, your employer will give you a **Form W-2.** This is a wage and tax statement. It shows how much money you earned during the past year. It also shows how much money was deducted for taxes.

You will get at least three copies of the W-2 statement. One is for you to keep. One goes to the federal government when you file your **income tax return.** And one goes to your state government when you file your state income tax return.

A tax return is a form used to state your income and figure out the amount of tax you should have paid for the previous year. You must file an income tax return by April 15 each year if your earnings were above a certain level.

When you send in your income tax return, include a copy of your W-2 statement from each employer you worked for that year. If the amount of taxes deducted from your pay was not enough, then you must send a check or money order to the government along with your return. But if too much money was deducted, you can look forward to a tax refund.

1 Control number 094863 C2L	22222	For Paperwork Reduction Act Notice, see back of Copy D. OMB No. 1545-0008	For Official Use Only ▶	
2 Employer's name, address, and ZIP code Memorial Hospital 219 Oak Street Riverside, GA 30902		3 Employer's identification number 13-1824180		4 Employer's state I.D. number 131824180
		5 Statutory employee ☐ Deceased ☐ Pension plan ☐ Legal rep. ☐	942 emp. ☐ Subtotal ☐ Deferred compensation ☐ Void ☐	
		6 Allocated tips	7 Advance EIC payment	
8 Employee's social security number 178-49-5237	9 Federal income tax withheld 2,917.00	10 Wages, tips, other compensation 26,520.00	11 Social security tax withheld 2,029.00	
12 Employee's name (first, middle, last) Alex Davis		13 Social security wages 26,520.00	14 Social security tips	
229 Heather Drive Monroe, GA 30909		16 (See Instr. for Forms W-2/W-2P)	16a Fringe benefits incl. in Box 10	
		17 State income tax 796.00	18 State wages, tips, etc. 26,520.00	19 Name of state GA
15 Employee's address and ZIP code		20 Local income tax 398.00	21 Local wages, tips, etc. 26,520.00	22 Name of locality Monroe
Form W-2 Wage and Tax Statement 199X 95-2830662 APR. I.R.S.		Copy A For Social Security Administration		Dept. of the Treasury—IRS

Alex's Form W-2 shows how much money he earned last year and how much money was deducted from his pay.

POINTS TO REMEMBER

In this section, you learned about the many things to do when starting a new job. Some of the most important include:

- learning as much as you can about your duties and about the company
- filling out a Form W-4
- learning how to use a time card or a timesheet
- calculating the deductions from your pay

TAKING ✓ STOCK

WORKING VOCABULARY

On a separate piece of paper, number 1 through 15. Then write the word or words that best completes each sentence. Note: there are more words than sentences.

adjustment period
allowance
association
co-pay
deductible
employee manual
enrollment form
exempt
Form W-2
Form W-4
head of household
HMO
income tax return
itemize
job description
orientation day
pay period
paystub
referral
time card
timesheet
traditional health care insurance
withholding form

1. A single parent who pays most of the household expenses is the _____ _____ _____.

2. Your _____ is the amount of money you pay for medical benefits before your insurance company starts to pay.

3. If you don't earn enough money, you can claim _____ tax status.

4. You can claim an _____ for each person who depends on your income.

5. During an _____ _____, you get used to a new job.

6. Employees are introduced to a new company and new jobs during an _____ _____.

7. You fill in the hours you work on a _____.

8. You send an _____ _____ _____ to the government by April 15.

9. You fill out a _____ _____ to let your employer know the number of dependents you're claiming.

10. The part of your paycheck that shows what deductions were taken out is the _____.

11. When you start a new job, your boss may give you a written _____ _____ that lists all of your duties.

The World of Work 81

12. An _____ _____ is a written guide that explains a company's rules.

13. The number of workdays an employee is paid for each paycheck makes up a _____ _____.

14. In an _____, a group of doctors organize to provide low-cost medical care.

15. You may need to fill out an _____ _____ when you sign up for health insurance benefits.

SKILLS FOR WORK

You have just started a new job. List five questions you would ask to avoid future mistakes.

1. _____
2. _____
3. _____
4. _____
5. _____

YOU DECIDE

You have just completed your first day at a new job. You didn't like it. Your co-workers were unfriendly and your boss was too busy to help you much. Would you stick with the job? Why or why not?

_____
_____

FINDING OUT MORE

You have started a new job. You have a few questions about your duties as well as company policies and rules. Your supervisor is out of town for several days, so you must find the information elsewhere. Answer the questions below about finding the information you need.

1. What form would answer questions about your duties?

   _____

2. What form will you have to fill out in order to be covered by the company's medical insurance?

   _____

3. What form will you have to fill out to tell the company how much your tax withholding should be?

   _____

4. What should you ask for and read to learn about vacations, hours, and other policies?

   _____
   _____

5. What form is attached to your paycheck to tell you what deductions were taken from your pay?

   _____

SECTION EIGHT

A JUGGLING ACT

"Hello, Ms. Delgado," Anna said to her supervisor on the phone. "I won't be able to come in again today. Jimmy's still sick. The doctor said that Jimmy should be well enough to go back to the child care center by Monday."

"Isn't today your fifth day off?" Ms. Delgado asked.

"Yes, it is," Anna said. "But since it's Friday, I shouldn't need any more time off."

"You're aware of the company's policy on personal time, aren't you?" Ms. Delgado asked.

"Yes, I am," Anna said. "I get four paid personal days a year."

"That's right," Ms. Delgado said.

"I don't have any other choice," Anna said. "I can't take Jimmy to the center while he's still sick."

"I understand," Ms. Delgado said. "I know it's hard to raise a child on your own. But Anna, we can't pay you for more than four personal days a year. We'll have to deduct the other day from your pay. I'm sorry."

Anna was quiet for a moment. Then she had an idea. "Could I make up the

day on a Saturday or a holiday? I really can't afford to lose the pay."

"I'm sure I can arrange that," Ms. Delgado said. "Just let me know which day you want to work, and I'll put you on the schedule."

"Thank you so much," Anna said. "After I get a babysitter, I'll let you know which Saturday I'll work." ■

Anna had to juggle many demands in her work and personal life. When you work, you may have to deal with many demands, such as:

- balancing your work and your family's needs
- arranging for child care
- managing your money
- handling illness
- dealing with stress

BALANCING WORK AND PERSONAL DEMANDS

Working parents like Anna have to play many **roles.** Anna is a daughter, a parent, an employee, a friend, and a sister. Each of these roles has its own set of demands.

Depending on the roles you play in life, the demands you face will vary. Some of the basic demands you might face in your work and personal life are listed below.

Work demands include:

- arriving on time
- working the required number of hours
- doing each task well
- working hard
- following company rules
- getting along with your supervisor and employer
- working well with co-workers
- traveling or working overtime
- growing with the job and taking on more responsibilities

Personal demands may include:

- meeting your own and your family's needs for food, clothing, and a safe home

Balancing work and personal demands may be difficult at times, especially if you have problems in one area.

- taking care of your children
- spending time with your spouse
- maintaining your health
- caring for sick family members
- getting education or training
- taking part in community or religious activities
- spending time with friends
- enjoying hobbies or relaxation

Most of these demands are more complex than they seem. For instance, consider the demand of providing food, clothing, and a safe home for you and your family. After a full day at work, a working parent like Anna might have to pick up her child, cook, and do laundry.

Later, Anna may have to go grocery shopping. Her father may need her to take him to the doctor. And all of this may happen the night Anna's boss asks her to work late.

In some homes, two adults share all of these tasks. But in many homes, a single parent must handle them alone. That single parent is usually the mother.

It's easy to see why working parents say there aren't enough hours in a day. And when there are problems in one area of life, it can make meeting demands in other areas even harder.

BEING A GOOD TIME MANAGER

How can meeting demands be made easier? The answer is managing your time. If you plan the hours in your day, you can get more chores done.

Follow these basic steps in managing your time:

1. Make a list of personal aims, or **goals,** that you want to achieve.
2. Put your goals in order of importance. This is called **setting priorities** (prye•OR•uht•eez).
3. Look at how you use time now and decide what can be improved.
4. Make a list of the goals you can achieve in the time you have.
5. Write up a schedule for using your time to reach your goals.

Let's take a look at how time management might work for Anna. She would start by thinking about what she wants to achieve. Her list would include **short-term goals.** Those are things that need to be done right away. They include finding a babysitter to watch Jimmy on a Saturday and helping Jimmy get well. She also must tell Ms. Delgado which Saturday she will work.

Anna also has **long-term goals.** These take more time to achieve and usually involve more planning. They include taking a business course at night school and finding child care for nights and for times when Jimmy is sick. Another of Anna's long-term goals is to get a promotion at work.

After Anna lists all of her goals, she puts them in order from most important to least important. She decides that helping Jimmy get well is her most important short-term goal. If Jimmy gets well, then she can return to work as planned.

The most important long-term goal is to find nighttime and emergency child care for Jimmy. That way Anna wouldn't need to miss any more work. She also could arrange to take the night school course. Taking that course might help her get promoted.

Listing Your Goals

Like Anna, you probably have short-term goals and long-term goals that you want to reach. List some of your goals on page 86. Include at least one goal from each area of your life—work and personal.

After you've listed your goals, then put the short-term goals in order of importance. Write the number next to the goal. Do the same for each long-term goal. Number 1 should be the most important goal. Number 5 should be the least important goal.

Short-Term Goals:

_____
_____
_____
_____

Long-Term Goals:

_____
_____
_____
_____

ARRANGING CHILD CARE

Working parents find that handling child care can be difficult and demanding. When parents aren't sure whether their children are getting good care, they can't keep their minds on work. They are busy worrying about their children. That's why it's so important to find a child care arrangement that you're happy and comfortable with.

Before Anna started working, she looked around for child care. She asked friends and relatives to recommend a good child care center. She also looked through the newspaper for child care and babysitting ads.

In addition, she got a recommendation for a good child care center in her area from her community's **referral service.** You can find out if your community provides this service by looking under the headings "Child Care" or "Day Care" in your phone book.

When you look for child care, you will see that there are three basic types of care. They include:

- **Care in the child's home.** A babysitter lives in the child's home or comes there every morning and leaves at night.
- **Family child care.** The child is taken to the child care provider's home every day. Several other children may be there as well.
- **Child care center.** The child and a group of other children are cared for by trained adults. The center may be in a school, community building, church or synagogue, or office building.

Each type of child care arrangement has good and bad points. Care in the child's home is convenient, but it's usually expensive. Family child care costs less than care in the child's home and allows children to be with other children. But most family providers don't have any training.

Child care centers are usually affordable and have a trained staff. In addition, centers must meet health, safety, and staffing requirements. But some centers are crowded and unpleasant for children.

Some families decide that child care facilities are not right for them. They plan their work schedules so that they do not need child care.

Anna's sister Jan works at home. She types letters for a mail-order

> ## Judging Child Care
>
> Before you choose a child care arrangement (or provider), make sure it's what you want and need. This list of questions can help you judge arrangements or providers.
>
> - When is care available?
> - What does it cost?
> - Can parents drop in any time? (They should be able to.)
> - Where is it located? How easy is it to get there?
> - How many children are cared for by each adult? (The numbers that are acceptable vary from state to state. You should check your own state's laws.)
> - What is each provider's experience or training?
> - Do you like the provider(s)?
> - Does each provider enjoy being with children?
> - Is there enough space?
> - Are there safe and interesting things to do both inside and outside?
> - Is the indoor space safe and clean?
> - Is it a cheerful place?
> - Do the children seem happy?
> - What happens if a child is sick?
> - How are emergencies handled?
> - How is misbehavior handled?
> - How are mealtimes handled?

business. The company she works for bought her a computer to use at home. Jan plans to keep working at home until her daughter starts first grade. Then Jan will work outside the home during the hours her daughter is in school.

Juan, a security guard at Anna's company, works the night shift, from midnight to 8 A.M. His wife works at a hospital from 3 P.M. to 11 P.M. Their hours allow them to take turns caring for their three young children.

HELPING LOW-INCOME FAMILIES GET CHILD CARE

Every year more parents that work need to find full-time child care for their children. But many of them can't afford to pay the high cost of full-time care.

There are government programs that can help parents who need affordable child care. Some of the programs set up inexpensive child care centers. Others help by paying all or part of the cost of child care. These programs are designed to help families who have low incomes.

Each state helps low-income families that need child care in different ways. To find out what kinds of help are available in your state and your community, look under the following headings in your local telephone book:

- Day Care Council
- Department of Health and Human Services
- Economic Opportunity Commission/Head Start
- Health and Welfare Council

If you call a government agency, ask if there are programs for child care and if the programs are full. If they are full, ask if you can fill out the forms and be put on a waiting list.

Choosing Child Care Providers

You are the parent of a two-year-old child. You have just been offered a full-time job that you want to take. However, you must find good child care for your child.

Which type of arrangement would you prefer: care in your home, family child care, or a child care center?

_____

Explain your answer._____

_____
_____
_____
_____

MANAGING YOUR MONEY

Another demand that can be difficult to deal with is handling money. Many people never have any money left over a few days after they're paid. If you fall into this category, try budgeting your money.

Budgeting your money, like managing your time, begins with setting short-term goals and long-term goals. Then you decide which goals are most important. The things you and your family *need* come first. The things you *want* come next. By breaking your spending habits into three categories, you can see how you have been spending your money.

After you've set goals, rated them, and learned how you manage your money, you make a plan or **budget.** The budget helps you control your spending and pay your bills.

Anna needed a budget. She had to be sure that she could afford to pay for night school and a babysitter. Anna's brother gave her a budget worksheet. This helped her figure out her budget. All she needed to do was fill in the numbers.

On page 89 there is a copy of the worksheet Anna used to figure out how she was spending her money. You will see that the money is divided into three categories:

- **Fixed expenses.** These are paid every month. They're usually the same amount, or **fixed.** An example would be your rent and utilities.
- **Variable expenses.** You have these once in a while, and the amounts vary. That's why they're called **variable** expenses. An approximate amount is used on the worksheet. An example would be clothing expenses.
- **Spending money.** This is the money you have left over after you pay all of your bills. This money may be used for entertainment, travel, or other enjoyment.

When Anna added up the worksheet, she realized that she was

spending about $5 more than she earned each month. That explained why she was always borrowing money from her brother. She decided to talk to him about managing her money. She knew he could help since he worked in the finance department of a big company.

Anna knew she couldn't change some of her expenses, such as rent or car insurance. But her brother showed her that she could control her spending. She decided to cut the amount of her pocket money in half. She also started using coupons at the grocery store.

These simple changes meant that Anna wouldn't spend more than she made. But Anna still had one problem. She hadn't saved any money. Anna's brother told her that everyone should save some money, even if it's only a small amount.

There are many reasons to save money. You may need it if there's an emergency, such as having to pay for a major repair. You can save for a child's education, a vacation, or a down payment on a car or home.

Anna thought that only people with high incomes saved money. She also thought that she could save only if she had money left over at the end of the month—and she never did.

Anna learned that all people who work should save some money. She decided to have money deducted from her paycheck and put into a savings plan. She would have $5 taken out each week at first. Later on, she would try to save more.

Like many people, Anna had let her

Anna's Sample Budget

Monthly Net Income $1,495

Fixed Expenses

Rent	$450
Car Payment	$150
Car Insurance	$90
Electricity	$30
Cooking Gas	$10
Telephone	$20
Credit Card Payments	$110
Gasoline	$30
Babysitter	$215
Food	$200
Savings	0
	TOTAL $1,305

Variable Expenses

Household Items	$20
Clothing	$40
Medical Costs	$35
Auto Repair	$20
Charity	$10

Spending Money

Entertainment	$30
Pocket Money	$40
	TOTAL $195

spending get out of control. In the past, she had paid for expensive items with a credit card. Now she was stuck paying $110 a month toward her bills. Almost $20 of that payment was **interest,** a fee that banks charge people for borrowing money.

Anna needs to change her spending habits. Once she has paid off her credit card bills, she should purchase fewer items with credit cards. And she should pay the entire amount of her credit card bill each month. That way she won't have to pay any more interest charges.

 Making a Budget

Suppose that you work and that your monthly net income is $1,200. You have the following expenses each month:

Food—$220

Rent—$630

Transportation—$110

Medical Costs—$70

Electricity—$30

Clothing—$25

Telephone—$25

Use what you have learned about managing money to complete the following budget. Fill in the figure for monthly net income first. Then divide the seven figures you have been given between the categories of fixed expenses and variable expenses. Then add up the figures to get a total and answer the questions that follow.

Monthly Net Income $ _____

Fixed Expenses

_____ $ _____

_____ $ _____

_____ $ _____

_____ $ _____

_____ $ _____

Variable Expenses

_____ $ _____

_____ $ _____

Total $ _____

1. How much money is left after you subtract "Total" from "Monthly Net Income"?

   _____

2. What would you use that money for?

   _____

HANDLING ILLNESS

Illness can throw many lives off balance. When Anna's son got sick, she had to take time off from work to care for him. Most child care centers won't care for sick children. Anna called her supervisor every day to keep her informed of the situation.

If you have to take time off because your child or another relative is sick, let your supervisor know right away. Your time off will probably be considered personal time. If you need a lot of personal time off, you may have to take a personal leave. You usually aren't paid for this time off.

Tell your supervisor if you will have to miss work for a long period of time. That way you won't be leaving the company or your department without help. Your supervisor may assign someone else to your job until you can return.

Most employees get a specific number of sick days per year. Find out how many you have *before* you need to take time off. If you're sick and must miss work, call your supervisor as soon as you know you won't be at work. If you're too ill to call, have another adult call.

If you will be out of work for a week or more, get a doctor's note explaining the illness or the injury. Employees who must miss several days or weeks of work may qualify for **disability pay** for a limited time.

If you are injured at work, let your supervisor know right away. You probably will have to fill out forms for your company and the insurance company. Injuries that force you to take time off may be handled differently from routine illnesses.

DEALING WITH STRESS

Most workers have many demands to handle. Those demands can add up to **stress.** You have probably felt stress at some time or other. It can make your palms sweat, your stomach churn, your heart pound, and your head ache.

Stress is the body's reaction to extreme demands placed on it. Many

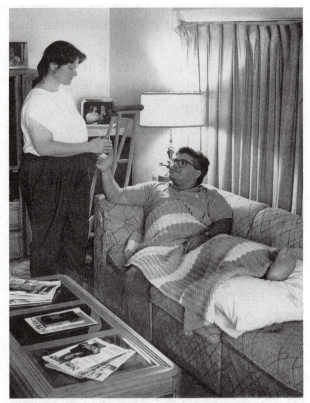

If you need extended time off from work because of an illness or injury, find out if you can qualify for disability pay.

situations cause stress. Stress can be caused by positive or negative experiences. Positive examples are getting married or starting a new job. Negative ones are getting injured or having a fight with your spouse.

There's no way to take all of the stress out of life. In fact, some stress is good for you. It can help you do your best. For example, athletes try harder when they are competing in a tough game. Stress causes a body chemical called **adrenaline** (uh•DREN•ul•un) to flow so that the athlete performs at his or her very best.

Stress can be a problem when it stops you from performing at your best. How can you keep that from happening? First, try not to take on

A Juggling Act

any more work or responsibilities than you can handle.

Second, prepare yourself for stressful situations that can't be avoided. Changes and problems happen in everybody's life. Remember how Anna's son got sick? That was bound to happen sometime. But it caused a lot of stress for Anna, because she wasn't prepared for it.

In the future, Anna will have someone available to care for Jimmy when he's sick. Because she will be prepared, she won't have to miss so much time at work. And then she won't have the added stress of worrying about her job.

How Well Do You Handle Stress?

How can you handle stress that you can't avoid? Here are some ways that people do it. Rate how often you do each one of the following on a scale of 1 to 5. Something that you do infrequently, you would number 1. Give something a 5 if you do it regularly. The higher your final score is, the better equipped you are to handle stress.

_____ **Exercise.** Do you walk, swim, dance, or do other exercise a few times a week?

_____ **Rest.** Do you get at least seven or eight hours of rest a night?

_____ **Communicate.** Do you talk to trusted friends or relatives about your feelings? If you have problems at work, do you discuss them with your supervisor or someone in the human resources department?

_____ **Compromise.** Do you compromise (KAHM•pru•myz) by giving in once in a while? (It's less stressful than fighting.)

_____ **Have fun.** Do you make time for hobbies and activities that you enjoy?

_____ **Get involved.** Do you have a worthy cause or an activity that gives you a lot of satisfaction?

_____ **Make your environment simpler.** Do you keep the noise and confusion at home and at work to a minimum? Or can you tune them out?

_____ **Avoid drugs and alcohol.** Do you know that these don't really relax you at all? (They just depress you and set you up for more stress.)

Too Much Stress

Are you under too much stress? Ask yourself the following questions to see if you are.

- Do you lose your temper easily?
- Do you have trouble concentrating?
- Do you get tired quickly?
- Do you have trouble relaxing or sleeping?
- Have you lost interest in people and activities that you used to enjoy?
- Do you worry a lot?
- Do you depend on alcohol or drugs to relax?

POINTS TO REMEMBER

In this section, you learned that people have to deal with many demands in their lives. Some of the most common include:

- balancing the demands of different roles
- managing your time
- finding a good child care arrangement
- learning to manage and budget money
- dealing with personal and family illness
- handling stress

■ TAKING ✓ STOCK ■

WORKING VOCABULARY

On the blank after each definition, write the correct word or words from the list. Then find the word in the puzzle on this page and circle it. The words can be forward or backward. Note: There are more words than definitions.

adrenaline	long-term goal
budget	referral service
compromise	role
disability pay	setting priorities
fixed	short-term goal
goal	stress
interest	variable

1. Expenses that are the same each month

   _____

2. Putting your goals in order of importance

   _____

3. You do this when you give in

   _____

4. A result of too many demands

   _____

5. Money the bank charges when you borrow money

   _____

6. A personal aim _____

7. Money that employees may qualify for if they miss several days or weeks of work for sickness or injury

   _____

```
v u r s u n l
a b o e v e a
d a d t e r o
i n e t r y g
s i f i x e d
a s a n e r o
b t e g l u d
i i n p o t c
l n o r g a o
i t e i l c m
t e l o a k p
y r d r d m r
p e h i r o o
a s k t d x m
y t j i e h i
t s s e r t s
m p s s i v e
```

A Juggling Act 93

SKILLS FOR WORK

Your sister has come to you for advice. She can't find enough time for all the demands she has in life as a wife, mother, and employee. You know the basic steps in managing time. Explain the five steps to her on the lines below.

1. _____
_____

2. _____
_____

3. _____
_____

4. _____
_____

5. _____
_____

YOU DECIDE

You have been feeling stressed for about a week. You have a new and difficult project at work. Your car broke down. And your son has been getting in trouble at school. How would you try to reduce the stress?

_____
_____
_____
_____
_____

FINDING OUT MORE

Talk to a friend or relative who has a child in child care. Ask him or her the following questions and write down the answers.

1. What type of child care is the child in?

_____

2. How did you find that provider or center?

_____

3. Are you happy with the arrangement?

_____

Why or why not?

_____
_____

4. What would you like to change about it?

_____

5. What advice would you give to someone looking for child care?

_____
_____

SECTION NINE
KNOWING YOUR RIGHTS

"Did you hear what Donna did?" Gail asked Joyce as they drove to the mall.

"No, what?" Joyce asked.

"She quit her job," Gail said. "She decided that she couldn't stand her boss coming on to her anymore."

"I'm glad she finally quit," Joyce said. "He's been making her miserable for months."

"You think she did the right thing?" Gail asked.

"Yes," Joyce replied. "What else could she do?"

"She could have stayed and fought it," Gail said. "Women don't have to take that kind of treatment."

"I don't agree," Joyce said. "You never win in these situations. No matter what she did, her boss would have found a way to make her suffer."

"But she shouldn't have let him get away with behavior like that," Gail said. "Now she's out of a job. And her boss will start coming on to the next woman he hires."

"But what can she do?" Joyce asked.

"She can get a lawyer, file charges against her boss, and take him to court," Gail said.

"That's easy to say," Joyce said. "But it's hard to win such cases. I say that Donna did the best thing. Now she can find a better job."

"Well," Gail said, "I think that's taking the easy way out. Women shouldn't be sexually harassed at work. And the only way to stop it is to fight it." ∎

Gail knew that Donna had certain rights. She felt that Donna should have stayed and fought against sexual harassment on the job. When you work, you have rights, too. In order to protect those rights, you should know:

- what basic rights employees and employers have
- what to do about unsafe working conditions
- how to deal with sexual harassment
- how to deal with discrimination
- what your right of privacy at work includes
- where to go for help if you feel that your rights have been denied

EMPLOYEES HAVE RIGHTS

Gail was correct. Donna has certain rights at work—including the right *not* to be **harassed** by her boss.

That right and others are the result of federal laws. Those laws protect employees against unfair treatment by their employers. Some of the rights that all workers have include the right to a safe workplace, the right to be free from sexual harassment, and the right to privacy. In addition, workers have the right to be considered for a job regardless of race, national origin, gender, sexual orientation, age, religious or political beliefs, or handicaps.

There are also many state and local laws that give workers additional protection against unfair treatment by employers. **Labor unions** may provide even more protection for their members in the workplace. That's because unions are organizations that bargain with employers on behalf of workers and their rights.

Getting Fair Treatment

Some situations at work may seem like they're illegal, when in fact they're only unfair. An employer who is fair follows some basic **principles**, or rules of behavior, when dealing with employees. They include:

- paying you on time
- explaining your duties and how to carry them out
- telling you about any changes in your duties or in company policies
- reviewing your performance with you at scheduled times
- telling you about chances for advancement in the company
- providing any training that you need to do your job

If you feel that you are being treated unfairly, talk to your supervisor. Explain the situation and ask for your supervisor's help or advice. For example, if you didn't get your performance review and raise on time, explain the situation to your supervisor. Then ask when you can expect the situation to be taken care of.

Handling Unfair Treatment

A co-worker comes to you with a problem. She tells you that her boss requires her to do personal chores for him. She has to balance his checkbook and buy his gifts for his family. She doesn't like doing those things. You know that what he's doing isn't against any laws. What would you advise?

_____
_____
_____
_____

EMPLOYERS HAVE RIGHTS TOO

Employers also have rights and **expectations** (eks•pek•TAY•shunz). That means employers can expect certain things from workers. For example, your boss has the right to expect you to do a full day's work for a full day's pay. That means you should get to work on time and do the work you're being paid to do. You are also expected to take only the allowed time for breaks and to work until the workday ends.

If workers are absent from work without a good reason, or if they arrive late or leave early, employers may subtract money from their pay for that time. This is called **docking.** Some employers fire employees for excessive lateness or absence.

When you accept a job, you agree to try to meet your employer's expectations by doing the job properly. If you don't perform up to expectations, you may be fired. If you commit a crime or don't do your work, then an employer will probably fire you right away.

If you break the terms of the **contract** between you and your employer, the employer may fire you. A contract is a legal agreement between two or more people. In addition, if you don't follow the policies in your company manual, your employer may fire you. For example, suppose your employee manual says that employees may have 10 sick days a year. If you have missed 15 days, your employer may fire you for taking too many sick days.

THE RIGHT TO A SAFE WORKPLACE

Under federal law, all workers have the right to work in safe surroundings. This law, the Occupational Safety and Health Act, aims to protect employees at work by setting safety and health standards. For example, to prevent accidents and injuries in factories, machinery should be in good running condition.

As a part of this law, employers must tell workers about any **hazardous** (HAZ•urd•us) materials in the workplace. And those dangerous materials must be properly labeled.

If you find hazardous conditions at work, tell your supervisor or employer about them immediately. If the problem isn't corrected, contact

Knowing Your Rights

the Occupational Safety and Health Administration (OSHA). This federal agency **enforces** job safety laws. It will send an inspector to make sure the law is carried out. If the law is being broken, the inspector may order an employer to correct hazards.

Keep in mind that, according to the law, an employer cannot fire you for contacting OSHA to report hazardous conditions.

 Safety on the Job

You have seen a damaged electrical plug on one of the computers at work. Who would you tell about it?

_____

_____

If, after a few weeks, nothing had been done to fix the plug, what would you do?

_____

_____

FREEDOM FROM SEXUAL HARASSMENT

Gail knew that there are federal laws to protect workers like Donna from mistreatment on the job. She felt that the unwelcome sexual advances and remarks from Donna's boss were against the law. The legal term for what was occurring is **sexual harassment.**

The federal Equal Employment Opportunity Commission (EEOC) defines sexual harassment as including sexual advances or other behavior of a sexual nature if:

- a worker must accept this behavior to keep the job
- an employer's hiring decision about an applicant or worker is based on how the person responds to improper advances
- the sexual behavior creates an unfriendly or difficult work environment or interferes with an employee's ability to work

Even though Donna's situation involved these problems, Joyce knew that proving sexual harassment can be difficult. Different people have different ideas about what kinds of sexual remarks and behavior are acceptable. For instance, someone who asks a co-worker for a date or makes a sexual joke may not be guilty of harassment.

If, however, you feel that you are being harassed at work, file a complaint right away. If your company has a formal procedure for handling these complaints, file your complaint there first.

If you are still being harassed, or if your company has no formal procedure, then file a complaint with the EEOC. The EEOC will review the facts and decide if sexual harassment has occurred. The EEOC will also consider how quickly the worker filed a formal complaint with the employer or with the EEOC.

In addition, the EEOC will consider whether the person who did the harassing has the power to hire, fire, or promote the worker who filed the

Getting Help

If you think that an employer has discriminated against you because of your race, file a complaint with the EEOC, the federal Civil Rights Commission, or a state civil rights agency. Nongovernment organizations can also help workers who have been treated unfairly. One of them is the American Civil Liberties Union (ACLU). Lawyers from this organization help people file lawsuits against employers who practice discrimination.

The National Association for the Advancement of Colored People (NAACP) is a nongovernment organization that defends blacks against discrimination.

Women often are targets of discrimination, too. If you have questions about laws that protect women against discrimination, you can call 9 to 5, National Association of Working Women, toll free at 1–800–245–9865.

---

complaint. If so, a court may order the employer to correct the problem and pay the worker for damages.

DISCRIMINATION ON THE JOB

In Section 5 you learned that, by law, employers cannot discriminate against you when you apply for a job. The same is true at work. Employers who discriminate against people on the job are breaking the law.

Discrimination may be racial, religious, or political. Or it may be based on national origin, age, handicaps, sexual orientation, or **gender,** which is whether a person is male or female.

Racial discrimination is quite common. For example, employers may not promote workers because of their race.

Laws require employers to base their decisions about hiring and promotions on qualifications. They must make decisions on the basis of workers' skills, education, experience, or general abilities.

 Dealing with Discrimination

Each situation below relates to a type of discrimination. After each one, write the type of discrimination that is involved. Then explain how you would deal with it.

1. An employer won't hire Carla because he thinks women are unreliable employees. What type of discrimination is this?

   _____

   If you were Carla, what would you do?

   _____
   _____

Knowing Your Rights 99

2. Mike, who is 50, applied for a job as a mechanic. The garage manager told Mike he wouldn't get the job because he is too old. What type of discrimination is this?

_____

If you were Mike, what would you do?

_____

3. Greg is Hispanic. He has worked for one company for 10 years. During those 10 years, his supervisor has only promoted less experienced white males. What type of discrimination is this?

_____

If you were Greg, what would you do?

_____

THE RIGHT TO PRIVACY

Another right that workers have is the right to privacy on the job. For example, if your employer lets you lock your desk, locker, or filing cabinets and doesn't have keys to them, none of those places should be searched. However, if you don't have locks on your desk, locker, or filing cabinets, then your employer can look in or search those places.

Some privacy issues have caused disagreement, or **controversy** (KAHN•truh•ver•see), in recent years. One includes the issue of testing workers for the virus that causes acquired immune deficiency syndrome, or AIDS. AIDS is a disease that has no cure and ends in the victim's death.

While you can't catch AIDS just by working with someone, AIDS is a problem for business. Medical treatment for AIDS costs tens of thousands of dollars per person. When companies employ people with AIDS, the costs of medical insurance and benefits increase. Because of this, some employers require that job applicants or workers be tested for HIV, commonly known as the AIDS virus. Other employers ask workers to volunteer to take these tests. Many people believe that this testing invades people's privacy.

If an employer requires that you be tested for the AIDS virus, your rights depend on the laws in the state where you work. In most states, you have to sign a form before your blood can be tested for this virus. The law also requires that the test results be kept secret. Most states treat AIDS as they treat other diseases and handicaps. An employer cannot fire or refuse to hire a worker only because he or she has the AIDS virus.

Drug testing is another controversial privacy issue. Many employers use drug tests to discourage drug and alcohol abuse by workers. Some people believe these tests invade workers' privacy. Others feel that the tests help to keep the workplace safe.

The U.S. Supreme Court has ruled that drug testing of some employees, such as people whose jobs involve

100   Section Nine

law enforcement or public safety, is legal. There are no federal laws on drug testing of other workers. However, some states and cities have passed laws that place limits on these tests.

Employers test workers for drug use because people under the influence of drugs can be dangerous. Employers are legally required to provide a safe workplace. Drug testing can help them do that. In addition to safety problems, workers who abuse drugs can cause other problems, such as poor work quality, conflicts, and theft or other dishonest behavior.

If you believe your right of privacy is being invaded at work, contact the American Civil Liberties Union or another state or local civil rights group in your area.

Taking a Drug Test

If you agree to take a drug test, the medical worker who takes your blood or urine should seal the samples with special tape. That way they cannot be tampered with. Make sure that this is done in front of you.

A lab will test the fluids for illegal drugs or certain prescription drugs. Evidence of some drugs, including marijuana, can show up as long as 28 days after they are used. Proof of other drugs may only show up for a few days.

Drug tests aren't always accurate. If an employee's blood or urine tests positive for drugs, he or she can ask to be given a second test to check this finding.

The Places to Find Help

In this section, you learned what to do in a lot of different situations. Read the situations below and explain what you would do to solve the workplace-related problem.

1. The only people getting promoted in your company are of the opposite sex. This has happened many times. You have more skill and experience than the people who got the promotions. What would you do?

   _____
   _____
   _____

2. Your company just bought some new equipment. You have been told that you must use that equipment today. But you haven't been taught how to use it. What would you do?

   _____
   _____
   _____

3. Your supervisor said he will fire you if you don't grant him sexual favors. You work in a small company that doesn't have a procedure for handling these types of complaints. What would you do?

   _____
   _____
   _____

Knowing Your Rights

4. You usually lock your locker at work because you keep personal belongings there. Your employer doesn't have a key to your locker. When you came to work today, your supervisor had opened your locker and found application forms for other jobs. He says he's going to fire you. What would you do?

_____
_____
_____
_____
_____

POINTS TO REMEMBER

In this section, you learned that there are many federal laws that protect workers' rights. Some of the most important are laws that:

- protect workers against mistreatment by their employers
- give workers the right to a safe workplace
- give workers the right to work free from sexual harassment
- allow workers the right to a job or promotion regardless of race, national origin, gender, sexual orientation, age, religious or political beliefs, or handicaps
- give workers the right to privacy

■ TAKING ✓ STOCK ■

WORKING VOCABULARY

Rewrite each sentence on a separate sheet of paper. Fill in the blank with the correct word or words from the list below. Note: There are more words than definitions.

contract
controversy
dock
drug testing
enforce
expectation
gender
harass
hazardous
labor union
principle
sexual harassment

1. An employer's _____ is that workers do a full day's work for a full day's pay.

2. Government agencies _____ laws.

3. The disagreement or _____ over drug testing has to do with the right of privacy.

4. A supervisor who won't promote a worker because she won't go out with him may be guilty of _____ _____.

5. A legal agreement between an employer and a worker is a _____.

SKILLS FOR WORK

You have a friend who feels that she is being discriminated against at work. She has asked you to explain the ways in which employers should treat their employees fairly.

List five things you would tell her.

1. _____
2. _____
3. _____
4. _____
5. _____

YOU DECIDE

You are applying for a job. The employer has asked you to take an AIDS test. Would you agree to take it?

_____

Explain your answer.

_____
_____
_____
_____

FINDING OUT MORE

The following laws protect workers' rights. Choose one law that you would like to learn more about.

Age Discrimination Employment Act of 1967
Civil Rights Act of 1964
Equal Pay Act of 1963
Fair Labor Standards Act
National Labor Relations Act of 1935
Pregnancy Discrimination Act of 1968

What law did you choose?

_____

After you choose a law, go to the library or look in an encyclopedia to find out more about the law. What does this law say?

_____
_____
_____

What right does this law protect?

_____

Does this law affect you? _____

If so, how? _____

_____

What was the source of your information?

_____

Knowing Your Rights

SECTION TEN
SUCCEEDING ON THE JOB

"I was pretty nervous at first," Rafael told his wife Teresa. "I wasn't sure how Ms. Taylor would react when I asked for a raise."

"What did you say to her?" Teresa asked.

"I told her that I wanted to talk about my job," Rafael said.

"What did she say?"

"She asked me if everything was alright," Rafael said. "I told her yes. Then she said that she had been meaning to talk to me for awhile."

"About what?" Teresa asked.

"Well," Rafael replied, "she said she knew I had been doing a great job. She told me how pleased she was with my work."

"Terrific!" Teresa exclaimed. "What happened next?"

"I mentioned how often I stayed late and worked weekends to meet deadlines."

"How did she react to that?" Teresa asked.

"She said that she had noticed how many weekends I worked these past six months," Rafael said. "And she said that I deserved to be rewarded for all my hard work."

"Well, then what?" Teresa asked.

"And then she said that I deserved a raise," Rafael said, with a smile.

"Did she tell you how much your raise would be?"

"She offered me another $50 a week—more than I was going to ask for!" Rafael said. "Let's take some of it and go out to celebrate." ■

Rafael was successful in his job. If you want to succeed in your working life, you should:

- have good work habits and a positive attitude
- cooperate with your supervisor and co-workers
- know how to ask for a raise or a promotion
- change jobs when it's the best way to advance
- leave a job on good terms with your employer

TIPS FOR SUCCEEDING

Rafael's supervisor was pleased with his performance. Rafael was given a raise because his employer valued his good work habits and positive attitude. These qualities can help you succeed at work.

Succeeding at your job means doing the best you can. In addition, successful people have positive attitudes about their jobs and their employers. They communicate with their supervisors, as Rafael did, and they get along with their co-workers.

Success on the job depends on small things, too. Your work habits may seem like minor details, but they affect your performance and the performance of others. Let's see which work habits can help you succeed.

- **Being on time.** You should get to work at the scheduled time, or even a few minutes early. Return from lunch and breaks on time, too. If you are going to be late or absent, call your supervisor.
- **Following rules and directions.** Certain rules and procedures have been made so that your job will be easier to perform and the company will run smoothly. Follow them to the best of your ability. If you see ways in which to improve procedures, give your suggestions to your boss.
- **Being reliable.** Always do whatever tasks you're given and finish them on time.
- **Being accurate.** Do your work as carefully as you can. If you make a mistake, admit it, and correct it if possible.
- **Being flexible.** When you're **flexible** (FLEKS•uh•bul), you adjust easily to new conditions. Many work situations require flexibility because conditions on jobs are always changing.
- **Cooperating with others.** Be polite and considerate of all the people you deal with at work.
- **Dressing with care.** Always look your best at work.

Your attitude also affects your performance. If you have a positive attitude, you enjoy your work and try to put your best foot forward. You look for the best in everything around you. If you have a negative attitude, you view work as a chore and you only do what you have to in order to keep your job.

Employers value workers who have positive attitudes. Such employees are cheerful, cooperative, and considerate. Since they get along with their co-workers, they help the company run more productively.

Why People Don't Succeed

Employers fire workers for many reasons. The most common reasons include the following bad habits and poor attitudes:

- not following directions or company rules
- lying
- stealing from the company
- being careless and making too many errors
- being lazy
- not finishing tasks
- not getting along with others
- coming to work late or leaving early
- being absent from work too much
- taking too many breaks or staying on breaks too long
- being unwilling to learn new tasks
- not making the effort to improve

Evaluating Your Habits and Attitude

You won't succeed at work unless you have good work habits and a positive attitude. Read the list of work habits that follow. Then rate yourself from 1 to 5 for each habit. Number 1 should be a habit that you rarely follow. Number 5 should be a habit that you always follow.

After you rate yourself, answer the questions below the list. Be honest with yourself.

- Am on time   Rating: _____
- Follow rules   Rating: _____
- Am reliable   Rating: _____
- Am accurate   Rating: _____
- Am flexible   Rating: _____
- Cooperate   Rating: _____
- Dress well   Rating: _____

Which habits did you rate yourself best in?

_____

_____

Explain why.

_____

_____

Which habits did you rate yourself worst in?

_____

_____

Explain why.

_____

_____

_____

How could you improve those habits?

_____

_____

_____

Would you say you have a positive attitude?

_____

Why or why not?

_____
_____
_____

YOU AND YOUR SUPERVISOR

Getting along with the people you work with can help you succeed. The most important person you will work with on the job will be your supervisor. That person will affect your success at work more than any other.

Your supervisor tells you how to do your job, answers your questions, and checks your work. Supervisors also judge your performance.

The key to getting along with your supervisor is having a positive attitude, doing your job well, and communicating often. Your supervisor expects you to be dependable, capable, and cooperative. He or she expects you to ask questions or seek advice whenever necessary.

Rafael and Ms. Taylor got along well because Rafael communicated openly with her. As a result, she praised him for his work.

As with Rafael and Ms. Taylor, you and your supervisor both need to keep the lines of communication open. Your supervisor needs to tell you how to do your job. He or she also needs to give you **feedback** about your work. That feedback may take place in an informal discussion or a scheduled performance review. At the same time, you need to talk to your supervisor about your work and any problems you may have.

Getting along with your supervisor can make your job more enjoyable. It can also help you succeed, since your supervisor is the one who is most likely to promote you.

YOU AND YOUR CO-WORKERS

Getting along with your co-workers also affects your success. If you have a good relationship with your co-workers, you will be happier at work. If you're happy, you'll do a better job. Supervisors want employees to get along so that their departments can run smoothly.

Rafael worked with many different people at his company. And he got along well with all of them. Rafael was also **supportive** of his co-workers. He helped them by working extra hours when they were sick or on vacation.

When you work with others as part of a team, you need to get along with everyone. In order to get the job done, your team must communicate and cooperate.

Getting along with your co-workers is easier if you follow a few simple rules. They may involve common sense, but they're important:

- Treat others the way you would like to be treated.

- Help others when they need it or when they ask for it.
- Show respect to workers who are more experienced or who know more than you do.
- Be pleasant, polite, and considerate.
- Don't talk about other people behind their backs.
- Don't talk down to people or be too critical.

Working with Other People

As a salesperson in a department store, Rafael had to deal with customers as well as co-workers. Many people have to work with customers, clients, or patients. Getting along with these people can affect your success at work.

Keep in mind the following points when you deal with customers, clients, or patients:

- Treat them the way you would like to be treated.
- Live by the motto "They are always right." Don't argue or get angry with them even if you know they're wrong.
- No matter how you're treated, remain pleasant, polite, and calm.
- Treat everyone with patience and consideration.
- Don't keep people waiting for service too long without a good explanation.
- If a person causes too many problems, refer him or her to your supervisor or someone in management.

HANDLING PERFORMANCE REVIEWS

How do you know if you're succeeding at work? Most people find out during performance reviews. At that time, supervisors tell workers how they're performing. Workers also have a chance to ask questions and share their feelings about their jobs, the department, and the company.

Some companies have formal performance reviews. The worker and the supervisor may both fill out a form and then discuss it. Or workers may fill out forms and then give them to supervisors to read and comment on. In other companies, the supervisors fill out forms and discuss them with individual employees.

When you are new to a job, your first few months or weeks at work may be a **probationary** (pro•BAY•shun•er•ee) **period.** That means that your performance is observed to decide whether you can do the work. At the end of the probationary or trial period, your supervisor judges your performance. If you have performed well, you will become a regular employee.

Whether you have a probationary period or not, you should have performance reviews. In many companies, employees are scheduled for reviews once a year. At that time, supervisors evaluate employees' work. Some companies give raises or promotions to workers who get good performance reviews.

No matter what type of job you have, you should have at least one review a year. If you're not sure what

At your performance review, you should take an active role in the review process by offering feedback about your job.

your company policy is, ask your supervisor. Find out when reviews take place, what will be evaluated, and how you will be judged.

A performance review is a two-way street. It involves both you and your supervisor. Your supervisor will give you feedback. You should openly discuss your feelings about your job and the company.

Don't be afraid of performance reviews. Instead, you should look forward to them. After all, they often are your only chance to express your feelings, ask questions, find out what you're doing right and wrong, and find out how to improve your performance.

HOW ARE WORKERS EVALUATED?

Performance reviews are different at every company. The evaluation forms used are also different. But most companies use the same **criteria** (kry•TIHR•ee•uh) to evaluate workers. That means that a worker's performance is measured against specific standards.

Some of the most common criteria include:

- **Skill.** Do you have a high enough level of skill and knowledge to perform your job effectively?

Succeeding on the Job   109

- **Quality of work.** Is your work correct, neat, and complete? Do you follow directions properly?
- **Time management.** Do you use your time well? Do you report to your supervisor when you complete tasks?
- **Reliability.** Do you arrive on time for work? Do you take only the allotted time for breaks and lunches? Do you complete work on time? Do you follow through on all work you're given? Do you work steadily, even with little supervision?
- **Dealing with people.** Do you respect authority? Do you get along with your co-workers? Do you work well with customers, clients, and patients? Are you cooperative and pleasant to work with?
- **Initiative.** Do you have the **initiative** (ih•NIHSH•ee•u•tihv) to take on new duties and challenges? Do you try to improve your performance? Are you flexible?

ASKING FOR A RAISE OR PROMOTION

People who succeed at their jobs want to be rewarded. Rewards usually come in the form of a raise or a promotion. When you get a raise, you get more money for doing the same job. When you get a promotion, you get a more responsible job. Usually, if you get a promotion, a raise comes with it.

A promotion is a sign of a worker's success. When people know that promotions are possible within a company, they put in extra effort. If you have a choice, avoid taking a job where promotions are limited. Otherwise, you may become trapped in a job that you've outgrown.

Most companies want to promote good employees because it's in their best interests to do so. Many companies give raises on a regular basis. In some cases, however, you may have to ask for a raise or promotion. Let's take a look at the best way to ask.

- **Schedule a time to speak to your supervisor.** Instead of interrupting your supervisor, wait until it's a good time for him or her to talk to you.
- **Choose a private place.** Don't ask in a public place where customers or other workers might overhear.
- **Pick the right time to make a request.** If there's a job opening or a new project, you may have a better chance of getting promoted.
- **Back up your request.** Show that you can handle the extra work and that you deserve it.

ARE YOU PROMOTABLE?

What makes a worker promotable? A worker needs to have certain qualities. Employers also want employees who can help the company be successful.

Here are some do's and don'ts for how you can do that.

DO...
- Carry out all your job tasks carefully and correctly.
- Follow the company's rules.
- Come in on time and work a full day and a full week.
- Keep yourself and your work space neat and safe.
- Care about the company and the product or service.
- Learn about the job and grow with it.
- Offer to take on extra work.
- Get along with your co-workers and supervisor.

DON'T...
- Make anyone's job harder.
- Break rules or have careless habits.
- Cause problems between other people.
- Cheat or steal.
- Refuse to change or to take on new tasks.
- Let personal problems get in the way of your job.

If you follow all of these tips for job success, you may get a promotion without even asking for it. Not all promotions involve moving into a more responsible job that already exists. Sometimes employers create positions that allow employees to put good skills to greater use.

When a supervisor clearly sees excellent work, he or she may decide to promote the worker who is responsible. A smart manager knows the importance of allowing a good worker to get ahead. And the more good work you do, the greater the chances your supervisor will notice and you will get promoted.

This worker is asking for a raise. What do you think she's doing right?

CHANGING JOBS

Many people advance to better jobs by changing jobs. In fact, most workers in the United States remain in the same job for only three and a half years.

Before you leave one job, it's always best to have another one lined up. Sometimes it takes a long time to find a new job. If you quit the job you have before getting a new one, you're likely to have trouble meeting your day-to-day expenses.

When you look for a new job, you will go through many of the same steps you followed on your first job hunt. You will read the help-wanted ads, make personal contacts, and go on interviews.

Succeeding on the Job

When you look for a new job, you will go through many of the same steps you went through to get the job you have now. Do you know what will be different?

When you look for a job this time, however, you will have new work experience to add to your list of qualifications. That experience may help you get the job you want.

When you decide to change jobs, it's best not to tell anyone at work. If your supervisor finds out before you're ready to leave, it may create problems for you.

Do all your job hunting on your own time, not on company time. Read the help-wanted ads in the newspaper and make telephone calls before or after work. Use your personal time to go on interviews, or arrange to have them during your lunch hour or before or after work, if possible.

While you are job hunting, act as if nothing is different at work. Keep up your good work habits and positive attitude.

WHEN IT'S TIME TO LEAVE

If you decide to leave your job, do so on a positive note. The way you **resign,** or quit, is important. After all, you may want to return to the company one day. Or you may need your supervisor or another manager to be a reference for you.

As soon as you know you're leaving, tell your supervisor. This may be difficult, especially if you like your job and the company. But the sooner your supervisor knows, the more time he or she will have to find someone to replace you. As a rule, try to tell your supervisor at least two weeks before you're leaving.

RESIGNATION LETTER

```
                            529 Whitehall Street
                            Boston, MA 02183
                            June 1, 199X


Mr. Carl Tsing, Manager
Minute Market
9283 S. Market Street
Boston, MA 02162

Dear Mr. Tsing:

I am writing to tell you that I am resigning
from my job as a salesclerk.

My last day of work will be June 18, 199X.
In July I will be moving to Arizona with my family.

I would be happy to help you train my replacement
during the next two weeks before I leave.

                            Sincerely,

                            Tom Harden
                            Tom Harden
```

Sometimes employers ask workers to stay. They may offer employees more money or a promotion if they stay. If that happens to you, weigh the pros and cons. Ask yourself two questions: How good is the offer? And how will staying affect my plans?

When you resign, explain why you're leaving. If there's a problem in the company or in your department, your supervisor will want to know. That way he or she can try to correct it.

After you resign, follow up with a **resignation letter.** See the feature on page 114 for tips on how to write one.

After you have told your employer that you are leaving, keep doing your best work. On your last day, turn in your keys and clear out your work space. Make sure the company has your address in case someone needs to ask you a question.

Resigning Your Job

When you write a resignation letter, you are formally telling your employer that you're quitting. When you do so:

- make the letter short and polite
- include the exact date that you are leaving
- explain your reason for leaving

Your Resignation Letter

You have been working at Antonio's, a local restaurant, for two years. Your supervisor is Marco Fiorelli. You've enjoyed the job and have learned a lot about waiting tables. Now you're leaving to go back to school to become a chef.

On a separate sheet of paper, write a resignation letter to your boss at Antonio's. Use the sample letter on page 113 as a guide.

POINTS TO REMEMBER

In this section, you learned about the many ways to succeed at work. Some of the most important include:

- having good work habits and a positive attitude
- getting along with your supervisor and co-workers
- knowing how to ask for a raise or promotion
- finding another job that offers better pay or chances for promotion
- resigning in a positive way

· TAKING ✓ STOCK ·

WORKING VOCABULARY

Fill in the blanks beside each definition with the correct word or words from the list below. When you complete the blanks, the circled letters will spell something you do before you leave a job. Note: There are more words than definitions.

criteria **initiative**
feedback **performance review**
flexible

probationary period **resignation letter**
resign **supportive**

1. _(_)_ _ _ _ _ _ _ _
   Specific standards that employers measure workers against

2. _ _ _ _ _ _ _ _ _ _(_)_
   You have this if you take on new duties and challenges

3. ◯ _ _ _ _ _ _ _ _
   A quality of people who help others

4. _ _ _ _ ◯ _ _ _
   A quality of people who adapt easily to change

5. _ _ _ ◯ _ _ _ _ _
   _ _ _ _ _ _
   A person who is quitting writes this

6. _ _ _ _ _ _ ◯ _ _
   _ _ _ _ _
   During this, your work is evaluated

7. _ _ _ _ _ _ What word do the circled letters spell?

SKILLS FOR WORK

Your boss has recently told you that you need to improve your work habits. List five things you might have to work on in order to improve.

1. _____
2. _____
3. _____
4. _____
5. _____

YOU DECIDE

You have accepted a job that pays better and is more interesting than the one you have now. When you tell your boss you're resigning, he offers to match the other job's pay and offers you a promotion.

Would you stay or go? _____

Explain your answer. _____
_____
_____
_____

FINDING OUT MORE

Talk to someone you know who has changed jobs at least one time. Ask this person the following questions. Then write down his or her answers.

1. Why did you leave the job you had?
   _____
   _____
   _____

2. If you resigned, how did you do it?
   _____
   _____
   _____

3. Did you leave the company on a positive note? _____

4. Why or why not?
   _____
   _____

5. Did that experience help you get a better job?
   _____
   _____
   _____

Succeeding on the Job

WORDS TO KNOW

A

abbreviate—to shorten
adjustment period—time for learning to adapt to new routines and new people
adjustment test—a test that determines whether a person has the personal traits a job requires; also called a personality test
adrenaline—a body chemical released when a person is under stress
allowance—on a Form W-4, the amount that can be deducted for the employee and each person who depends on the employee
application letter—a letter that aims to persuade an employer to interview a job applicant
apprentice—an on-the-job trainee who earns wages while learning a trade
aptitude test—a test that measures a person's natural abilities for performing and learning certain kinds of tasks
association—an organization or group of persons who have common goals or interests

B

background skill—a skill used in many areas of life that can help you on the job
basic skill—a basic ability, such as reading
beneficiary—a person named to receive money from an insurance policy if an employee covered by the policy dies
blind ad—a help-wanted ad that does not include the name, address, or telephone number of the company
body language—certain messages a person's body sends, communicated by expressions, gestures, and posture
box number—a number at a newspaper's address where job applicants reply to ads
budget—a plan for spending and saving money

C

civil rights—rights guaranteed to people by the U.S. Constitution, such as the right to equal treatment under the law
classified—the section of a newspaper where employers place ads for job openings
closing—a word or phrase put at the end of a letter before a person's signature, such as "Sincerely," or "Yours truly"
commission—pay that is a percentage of the amount of sales a salesperson makes
commute—to travel to and from a job
compromise—to give up part of your plans and find an alternative or make concessions
constitutional rights—see *civil rights*
contract—a formal, written agreement between two or more people
controversy—a dispute or disagreement
conviction—a judgment of guilty for a criminal offense
co-pay—a part of the cost of a health care plan that workers are required to pay
criterion—a standard, rule, or test by which something is judged or measured; plural: criteria

D

data—information, such as facts, numbers, or files
deductible—a part of medical expenses that a person must pay before medical insurance benefits begin
deduction—a sum of money that is subtracted from an employee's gross income for taxes, health insurance, and more
disability pay—a benefit received by a worker who is out of work for a long period of time due to illness or injury
discriminate—to treat a person differently because of race, religion, national origin, ancestry, age, sex, or handicap
dock—to subtract money from a worker's pay for missing work without a good reason
drug testing—testing procedure used to determine if a person is abusing drugs or alcohol

E

employee manual—a written guide that explains a company's rules and structure, fringe benefits, promotion procedures, and more
enforce—to make sure a law is carried out
enrollment form—a form an employee fills out when signing up for health insurance benefits
Equal Employment Opportunity Commission (EEOC)—an agency that enforces federal civil rights laws
exempt—free from a rule or obligation that

applies to others; an employee who doesn't earn enough money to owe federal income tax may claim this status

expectation—something that is expected of a person

feedback—a person's response to another person's message

fixed—something that is the same, such as fixed expenses

flexible—adjusting easily to new conditions

flextime—a type of plan that allows workers to have flexible working hours, within limits

Form W-2—a wage and tax statement that an employee receives each January; shows how much money was earned during the past year and the amount deducted for taxes

Form W-4—a form that determines how much money will be deducted from a person's salary for federal and other income taxes; also called a withholding form

fringe benefit—payment to employees in a form other than money, such as health insurance or paid vacation time

gender—related to whether a person is male or female

gestures—motions made with the hands

goal—an aim that a person wants to achieve

greeting—a phrase that opens a letter, such as "Dear Mr. Smith"

gross pay—the pay a worker earns before any deductions are taken out

harass—to bother a person with improper remarks and actions

hazardous—dangerous

head of household—a claim allowed on a Form W-4 by a single parent who pays all household expenses

Health Maintenance Organization (HMO)—a group or association of doctors organized to provide low-cost medical care; works on the idea that making regular visits to the doctor prevents illnesses that result in expensive bills

help-wanted—an announcement or ad placed by an employer looking for help

hygiene—good health and cleanliness

income tax—a portion of a person's income that is paid to the federal and state governments

income tax return—a form used to figure out how much tax you should have paid for the past year

index—a list at the front of a newspaper that tells what's in each section

initiative—the desire to take on new responsibilities or challenges, or to start a task or project on one's own

insurance policy—agreement that provides money to someone an employee has chosen, in the event that the employee dies while working for the company

interest—(1) a fee that banks charge people for borrowing money; (2) an activity that you enjoy or that you like to talk or read about

interview—a meeting between an employer and a job applicant to determine if an applicant is right for a job

itemize—to list income tax deductions by individual items

job description—a list of a job's responsibilities and everyday duties

job sharing—a situation in which two people share the same full-time job, and each person works part-time

labor union—an organization that bargains with employers on behalf of workers

long-term goal—a goal that may take some time to achieve and usually involves planning

manual labor—using one's hands as part of a job

net pay—the amount of pay a worker takes home after taxes and deductions have been taken out of gross pay; also called take-home pay

objective—a brief statement that describes what kind of job a person is looking for

Words to Know 117

orientation day—a day when new employees learn about their new job and company; often before the first working day

pay period—the number of work days an employee is paid for on each paycheck
paystub—a written record that comes with a paycheck and shows the deductions from gross pay
performance review—an evaluation of a worker's performance; it's often an annual, formal meeting between an employer and an employee
personal trait—an individual quality of a person
personality test—see *adjustment test*
personnel department—a department in charge of hiring for a company; also called department of human resources
potential—expressing possibility or capability
principle—a rule of behavior
probationary period—the time during which a new employee's performance will be observed to determine if he or she is capable of doing the work
profanity—obscene or disrespectful language
promotion—an advancement within a company

qualification—knowledge, experience, or skill that makes a person suitable for a job

reference—a person, such as a past employer, who can tell an employer about a job applicant's character or work performance
referral—the action of directing someone elsewhere for information or aid
referral service—a place where a person can get a recommendation for a service needed, such as child care
resign—to quit a job
resignation letter—a letter that an employee writes to inform an employer that he or she is leaving a job
resume—a detailed, written summary of a job applicant's background and qualifications provided to an employer
role—a part played by a person, such as worker, parent, or friend

salary—the amount of money a job pays
set priorities—to put goals in order of their importance
sexual harassment—improper advances or remarks of a sexual nature from a supervisor or co-worker
shift work—work period divisions that are common in industries operating 24 hours a day
short-term goal—a goal that may be reached right away
skill—an ability developed by training and experience
slang—informal language
strength—something productive a person has to offer, such as a talent or technical skill
stress—mental and physical tension or strain
supportive—giving support or help

take-home pay—see *net pay*
talent—an ability that a person has and can perform without much difficulty
technical skill—a skill that is particular to a specific job, such as typing
time card—a form that helps employees keep track of the hours and days they work
time clock—a device that records the times when workers begin and finish working each day
timesheet—a form on which employees write the hours and days they have worked
tip—money that a satisfied customer usually leaves for service workers, such as waiters and waitresses
trade-off—a giving up of some things you want in order to get other things you consider to be more important
traditional health care insurance—a type of insurance that protects people from major medical expenses and loss of income due to health-related problems

variable—something that changes, such as variable expenses

withholding form—see *Form W-4*
work value—a feature of a job that is important to a person, such as work environment

ANSWER KEY

If answers are not provided, then answers will vary.

SECTION 1: GETTING READY FOR WORK

Working Vocabulary
Page 11

1. basic skills
2. talents
3. background skills
4. qualifications
5. interests

Skills for Work
Page 12

Any five of the following: talents, basic skills, technical skills, background skills, education and training, and work experience.

SECTION 2: FINDING A JOB LEAD

What's in an Index?
Page 16

1. Section E
2. on page 1 of Section E
3. in the Business section, or Section B
4. Autos, Help Wanted, and Real Estate

What's in an Ad?
Page 18

CLERICAL Fast-growing company needs full-time clerical personnel with 1 to 3 years office experience. Immediate openings. Send letter to: B1369 Austin Newspapers.

1. clerical jobs
2. no
3. by sending a letter to the box number at the newspaper
4. 1 to 3 years of office experience
5. immediately

Using the Yellow Pages
Page 19

1. automobile repairs
2. child care— child care centers
3. real estate—management companies
4. retail—stores

Working Vocabulary
Page 21
Across:
2. box number
3. index
6. abbreviate
7. apprentice

Down:
1. personnel
2. blind ad
4. interview
5. classified

Skills for Work
Page 22

Talking with people you know; responding to help-wanted signs or announcements; replying to help-wanted ads; calling employers; contacting state employment services.

SECTION 3: APPLYING YOURSELF

Working Vocabulary
Page 35

1. references
2. greeting
3. slang
4. objective
5. closing
6. resume

```
e r a u b d a s g t
h v k l e m t o r o
r e f e r e n c e s
a n e p e w o i e t
d c l o s i n g t e
a u o t u o k n i s
w i l l m e m a n d
u t j e q i l g o
b e z k o n s s e v
e v i t c e j b o w
```

Skills for Work
Page 36

1. your Social Security number
2. the names, addresses and dates of schools you attended
3. the names, addresses, and telephone numbers of your last three employers
4. the pay for your last three jobs
5. the names, addresses, and telephone numbers of three references
6. your visa number and the date it expires, if you're not a U.S. citizen

SECTION 4: Q & A: THE JOB INTERVIEW
Working Vocabulary
Page 46

1. personality test and adjustment test
2. body language or gestures
3. personal traits
4. potential

SECTION 5: A WINNING INTERVIEW
Working Vocabulary
Page 56

Across:
3. constitutional rights
5. hygiene
7. discriminate

Down:
1. civil rights
2. manual labor
4. EEOC
6. profanity

SECTION 6: I'LL TAKE IT
Reading a Map
Page 62-63

1. Route 1 east to 395, then back to 1, then north on 32 (also, could say Route 1 to 395, then southeast on 85 and south on 32)
2. around 6 miles
3. Route 1 east to 395, then north to 95, and finally to 184
4. between 13 and 14 miles
5. the job in New London would be easier because it's about half the distance of the other job

How Much Would You Make?
Page 64

Job #1:
gross pay = $300
take-home pay = $240
Job #2:
gross pay = $350
take-home pay = $280
Job #3:
gross pay = $297.50
take-home pay = $238.10

Working Vocabulary
Page 67

1. job sharing
2. trade-off
3. flextime
4. take-home pay
5. beneficiary
6. gross pay
7. salary

Skills for Work
Page 67

Any five of the following: where the job is located; what hours you would work; how much money you would make; what benefits you would get; how much money you would spend on work-related items; the chance for advancement.

SECTION 7: THE WORLD OF WORK
Understanding a Time Card
Page 76

1. $8 1/2$ hours
2. 9 hours
3. 8 hours
4. 42 hours

Working Vocabulary
Page 81-82

1. head of household
2. deductible
3. exempt
4. allowance

5. adjustment period
6. orientation day
7. timesheet
8. income tax return
9. Form W-4
10. paystub
11. job description
12. employee manual
13. pay period
14. HMO
15. enrollment form

Finding Out More
Page 82

1. job description
2. enrollment form
3. Form W-4
4. employee manual
5. paystub

SECTION 8: A JUGGLING ACT

Making a Budget
Page 90

Monthly Net Income	$1,200
Fixed Expenses	
Food	$220
Rent	$630
Transportation	$110
Electricity	$30
Telephone	$25
Variable Expenses	
Medical Costs	$70
Clothing	$25
Total	$1,110

1. $90

Working Vocabulary
Page 93

1. fixed
2. setting priorities
3. compromise
4. stress
5. interest
6. goal
7. disability pay

```
v  u  r  s  u  n  l
a  b  o  e  v  e  a
d  a  d  t  e  r  o
i  n  e  t  r  y  g
s  i  f  i  x  e  d
a  s  a  n  e  r  o
b  t  e  g  l  u  d
i  n  n  p  o  t  c
l  n  o  r  g  a  o
i  t  e  i  l  c  m
t  e  l  o  a  k  p
y  r  d  r  d  m  r
p  e  h  i  r  o  o
a  s  k  t  d  x  m
y  t  j  i  e  h  i
t  s  s  e  r  t  s
m  p  s  s  i  v  e
```

Skills for Work
Page 94

1. Make a list of your personal goals.
2. Put your goals in order of importance.
3. Look at how you use time now and decide how to make improvements.
4. Make a list of goals you can achieve in the time you have.
5. Write a schedule.

SECTION 9: KNOWING YOUR RIGHTS

Safety on the Job
Page 98

Tell your supervisor or employer. If the problem is not corrected, contact OSHA.

Dealing with Discrimination
Page 99

1. gender discrimination
2. age discrimination
3. racial discrimination

Working Vocabulary
Page 102

1. expectation
2. enforce
3. controversy
4. sexual harassment
5. contract

Skills for Work
Page 103

Any five of the following: pay them on time; explain their duties; tell them about changes in duties or policies; review their performance; tell them about chances for advancement; provide any training they need.

SECTION 10: SUCCEEDING ON THE JOB

Working Vocabulary
Page 114-115

1. criteria
2. initiative
3. supportive
4. flexible
5. resignation letter
6. performance review
7. resign

Skills for Work
Page 115

Any five of the following: being on time, following rules and directions, being reliable, being accurate, being flexible, cooperating with others, dressing with care.